CW00796576

The Bull and The Ban – The Book

Catherine Tosko

Foreword by Alexander Fiske-Harrison

Bullfight critics ranked in rows
Crowd the enormous Plaza full;
But there's only one who knows
And he's the man who fights the bull.

Dominic Ortega

The Iberian Peninsula

Andalusia

- Catalonia
- (Rest of) Spain
- Portugal
- ○ Barcelona

Foreword by Alexander Fiske-Harrison

In this book you will find the entire range of views on bullfighting represented in a series of interviews – from those who are completely against it to those who are completely for it – backed by the strongest arguments they can give. And although in my own interview I give the views I have come to hold after two years in Spain researching my own book on the subject – namely against any form of ban, but with grave misgivings about the cruelty of the activity – I have actually inhabited each position given at different times along the way.

As a child I joined both Greenpeace and the World Wide Fund for Nature because of a deeply felt and typically British love of animals, and even began my studies at university as a biologist with hopes of working in big game conservation. However, I was always much more sanguine than the representatives of Equanimal interviewed in the book. The realities of conservation and ideals of animal rights part company quite quickly. A classic example of this is on culling, be it badgers in the English countryside or elephants on the Savannah plains.

It was not until I saw my own first bullfight, and saw the possibilities of beauty in it, that my mind began to turn, although the cruelty was still clear to me. I also saw the staggering courage of the bullfighter, as described in the brief remarks of the matador Francisco Rivera Ordóñez about his father's death on the horns of a bull. Rivera's own strange relationship of love with the bull, and his views about his own death, are well summed up in the words of that great American *aficionado* of the bullfight, Ernest Hemingway, when he was writing about Rivera's grandfather Antonio Ordóñez:

"Any man can face death, but to be committed to bring it as close as possible while performing certain classic movements and do this again and again and again and then deal it out yourself with a sword to an animal weighing half a ton which you love is more complicated than just facing death. It is facing your performance as a creative artist each day and your necessity to function as a skilful killer."

Of course, the first problem for the Anglo-Saxon – as the Spanish refer to all English-speakers – mindset is the immense conflict with our sense of fairplay. Although 533 famous *toreros*, 'bullfighters', have had their deaths recorded in the annals of *la corrida de toros*, 'the running of bulls', since 1700 (which begs the question of how many lesser known toreros' lives have ended the same way), this is not meant to be a fair fight or even a sport at all. Our translations of these Spanish words into English are part of the problem with our perception of it: "bull-fight" is a 17th Century English word co-opted from our own foul habit of bull-baiting with dogs, and the term bullfighter derives from it.

You do not fight a bull, as my fellow torero Frank Evans says, but induce it to run – *correr* – past you with the dextrous use of the cape, using passes from the dance-book of bullfighting that has evolved over the past three centuries, striving for a physical elegance which results in a series of *tableaux* of man and bull designed to engage and alter the emotions of the crowd, until the exhausted bull is dispatched with the sword to complete the three-act tragic form of the drama.

However, I am not pretending that the *corrida* is done from beginning to end by a single man. Yes, he is first in the ring to face the bull with the large pink cape when it is fresh and untouched, but then it faces the *picador* on the armoured horse – as the picador Miguel Perea describes in his interview – and then the *banderilleros* with their three pairs of multi-coloured barbed sticks, who are, like the picador, all employees of the matador – although some matadors still place their own, like my friend Juan José Padilla. Padilla who was so gruesomely gored while doing so in 2011 that the image flashed around the world's media. (He has since returned to the *plaza de toros* in triumph, even with only one eye.)

Only after this does the matador return to the ring with smaller red cloth – the *muleta* – and the sword to begin the intricate dance for which the corrida is famed. There is nothing fair here, just as there is not at the abattoir, and even if the bull were to kill the matador, another matador would take his place.

Whether or not you find this as something moving or something barbaric, something outdated or simply something bizarre, comes down to which protagonist on the sand you find yourself identifying with, as the author Jason Webster notes in his interview.

The very best expression I have ever read, in Spanish or English, of the purpose of the corrida comes from the pen of the great American filmmaker and actor, Orson Welles, a friend of both Hemingway and Ordóñez in whose house his ashes now lie interred:

"What it comes down to is simple. Either you respect the integrity of the drama the bullring provides or you don't. If you do respect it, you demand only the catharsis which it is uniquely constructed to give... What you are interested in is the art whereby a man using no tricks reduces a raging bull to his dimensions, and this means that the relationship between the two must always be maintained and even highlighted. The only way this can be achieved is with art. And what is the essence of this art? That the man carry himself with grace and that he move the bull slowly and with a certain majesty. That is, he must allow the inherent quality of the bull to manifest itself."

Views contrary to this about the corrida have been around for as long as it has, although it is only relatively recently that animals have been the centre point of the argument. When Pope Pius V tried to ban it in 1567, he saw it as a unnecessary endangering of Christian souls in a way similar to duelling or suicide. However, by the nineteenth century this had changed. *La Sociedad Protectora de Animales y Plantas de Cádiz* was founded in 1872, but long before that was the British Society for the Prevention of Cruelty to Animals, founded in 1824, and gaining its Royal warrant from Queen Victoria in 1840 to become the RSPCA the year after it banned Britain's own Pamplona-style running of the bulls through the streets of Stamford, Lincolnshire in 1839. (The American Society for the Prevention of Cruelty to Animals was founded in 1866.)

These battle lines are drawn by two interlinked issues, as the interviews show: how we view Death, and how we value animals. In what the Spanish call the Anglo-Saxon world we view animals through a glass darkly, or – to put it less poetically – through broken lenses. This is shown in our language itself. We do not eat cattle or calves, but "beef" or "veal"- and we do so at a rate of three million cattle a year in Britain and thirty four million a year in the US.

And we do not do so out of need, but because we like the taste, in spite of the fact that with our ever swelling obesity crisis it has a measurably negative nutritional value, to say nothing of the environmental damage cattle-farming causes. And to put it plainly, these animals die for the entertainment of our palates, and at the expense of our waistlines, wallet and wild spaces. In the words of the animal rights philosopher Mark Rowlands, reviewing my own book in *The Times Literary Supplement*:

"The lives of fighting bulls are better than those of beef cattle, and death in the ring is no worse than death in a slaughterhouse. Let us accept this."

The reason we are happy to kill this many animals after an inferior quality *and* quantity of life – beef cattle average 18 months mostly in corrals, while fighting bulls range wild in forested wilderness for between 4 and 6 years at one third the population density of British beef cattle – is because we are so distantly separated from their deaths. In Great Britain, the move away from an agricultural economy by means of an "industrial revolution" began in the late 1700s, and in the US not long afterwards. Spain, on the other hand, was still massively agricultural as late as 1900, with the interesting exception of Catalonia.

Meanwhile, the great change in Britain and America's relationship with animals can be seen in two of the iconic books of that period, Rudyard Kipling's *The Jungle Book* and Jack London's *Call Of The Wild*, in which animals don't just have feelings and desires, but every human cognitive trait from self-consciousness to language. Back in the real world, science only attributes self-consciousness to primates, cephalopods – whales, dolphins and porpoises – and the elephant (admittedly via the crude 'Gallup Test'). While language is a controversial area of study in which research is almost exclusively with highly trained great apes (another area I have written about).

It is this historical difference between our countries that gives the biggest clue of all to the difference in mindset over our "four-legged friends" (a phrase which we only adopted in the UK after hunting to extinction the less than friendly wolf, bear and wild boar).

When Paul McCartney of the Beatles said that if abattoirs had glass walls we'd all be vegetarians, he didn't realise that this doesn't mean that it is wrong to kill animals, just as animals kill each other. What it means is that we have become so far distant from our means of food production we can no longer stomach the reality along with the product. It is a result of us becoming unhealthily sensitive to the natural conclusion to life – death – not of our having progressed to a more advanced or civilised state of being or society.

The truth of this is clearer when you think about one of the most successful television formats in either the UK or US, the nature documentary. How many shots of lions bringing down buffalo has David Attenborough provided his charming narration for? And how much footage of the lions beginning to eat the buffalo while still alive – which such a large and dangerous mammal almost invariably is – remains on the cutting room floor of the BBC's Natural History Unit?

In sun-blasted rural Spain, though, things are – still – different. As the greatest Spanish poet of the twentieth century, Federico García Lorca put it in his essay on *duende*, the dark spirit which is central to the corrida's cousin flamenco:

"It is not an accident that all Spanish art is linked to our mountains, with their thistles and sharp stones...

In all other countries death is an end. It arrives and the curtains are drawn. In Spain, no. In Spain they open. Many people there live indoors until the day they die and they are taken out into the sun. A person dead in Spain is more alive than dead than anywhere else in the world...

Spain is the only country where death is the national spectacle, where death plays long trumpets at the arrival of spring, and his art is always ruled by a sharp duende who has given it its difference and its quality of invention."

This is a strong note, and not one with which it is easy for everyone to agree. However, I think that no one can deny, even if they admire the sentiment – and sentimentality – of the voices of the group Equanimal interviewed in this book, that part of the source of their anti-bullfighting feeling is a deep terror of death:

"I don't want to be killed, first slow or fast, no one wants to be killed, no individual wants to be killed, where it's a quick death or slow death, of course if I'm going to be killed I prefer a quick death of course, but in the first case I don't want to be killed – so a bull is the same."

The other statements of Equanimal make them seem not so much "sinister", as Frank Evans says, but plain wrong. They claim that when bulls are reared wild they are completely peaceful, even though bull-breeders accounts books can tell you of the expensive losses of animals caused by fights between bulls, just as there are in African buffalo herds.

They also speak of the pain of the bull after its spinal column has been severed, even though this cuts both motor **and** sensory neurones: no more movement **and** no more pain. They even claim that the bull is warning the rest of his herd to flee when he vocalises in the plaza (something I saw only twice in the three hundred bulls researched for my book). He is, in fact – like any social animal – calling for assistance. Something no less piteous but let us at least try to stick to the facts.

The Spanish bull, whose life is better in so far as it is what I would choose for myself, has his injury in the ring justified for me by this culturally embedded art form that is also a ritual – a tragic play that contains a sacrifice.

All of this, of course, should be taken in light of the second half of the title of this book (in English), "the ban" of Spanish-style bullfighting in Catalonia. Note that the ban does not include the *correbous* and *correfoc*, in which every animal's most dreaded instinctive enemy, fire, is made to envelop and enshroud its head, and it is then run wild and insane among a taunting crowd. If anyone ever wanted to see the machination of politics dressed as the purity of ethics, it is contained in Article 6 of that ban exempting these two distinctly Catalan hobbies. Something the politicians quoted within seem to tacitly acknowledge when pinned down by the interviewer's questions.

The concrete proof that the ban was indeed largely political is also contained in the voting statistics themselves. In the Catalan parliament in July 2010, three-quarters of the votes in favour of the ban came from Catalan nationalist parties, while both the Spanish national parties – conservatives **and** socialists – accounted for three quarters of the votes against the ban. It was passed in the end by 68 votes to 55, with 9 abstentions. It is the socialist party's voice – banned at the time of Franco – that should tell you that the rest of

Spain does not see bullfighting as part of the old totalitarian Spain.

However, I am aware that I am now espousing views which I have come to hold, for better or worse, rather than letting you make up your own mind. The interviews here provide an excellent starting point for you to do just this.

Alexander Fiske-Harrison's book, *Into The Arena: The World Of The Spanish Bullfight* was published by Profile Books in the UK in 2011, and was shortlisted for the William Hill Sports Book of the Year later that year.

Introduction by Catherine Tosko

The year I moved to Spain was the year bullfighting was banned in Catalonia. Catalonia is the right shoulder of the Iberian Peninsula and an autonomous region of Spain, although a great deal of Catalans consider Catalonia to be a separate country to Spain, with its own language, Catalan, and own parliament, the *Generalitat*. Catalans make up a sixth of all Spaniards, and therefore Catalonia's vote on any subject should give the rest of the European Union a good indication of what Spaniards want. But this is not the case.

In 2009, when an independent platform in Catalonia calling themselves Prou ("Enough" in Catalan) banded together on the streets of Barcelona and collected over 180,000 validated signatures to enter a white paper, known as an ILP (Initiative of Popular Legislation) to the *Parlament de Catalunya* to prevent bullfights from taking place in bullrings in any plaza within Catalonia for animal rights reasons. Nobody really took any notice until, in July 2010, during a sleepy and fairly empty open parliamentary session, the Catalan Parliament voted, and to most people's amazement, passed the ILP to ban bullfighting.

There was an outcry so huge even those Spanish citizens with not an iota of interest in *los toros* began standing up to be counted, taking sides; even the King of Spain confirmed his *aficion*. As matador Francisco Rivera Ordóñez told me, it's when bullfighting is attacked, that people come to its defence. The bullfighting community declared that this vote was a political move: to quell the separatists who hated anything Spanish. This was a conspiracy, towards a dictatorship. Indeed, at the time of the vote, the then President, José Montilla had done less well than expected in elections, forming instead a ruling coalition with other parties, meaning Catalans had voted for one set of ideals and got another: a mixed bag of policies, including a wobbly stance on bullfighting.

However, Catalan separatists tell me the end of bullfighting in Catalonia is a pro-Catalan move, to promote modern decency and rights for all, including animals. They stumble over the reason for the added clause which means the Southern Catalan versions of bull festivities, the correbous and correfoc are not banned, left intact maybe because a prohibition of these popular bull baiting activities would 'move' votes in Catalonia in the 'wrong' direction; in other words, away from the more progressive, separatist parties. The *taurinos* argue that this vote was therefore not about animal rights, and more about appearing progressive, to enter the EU as a new and modern country, as Catalonia. That this ban actually has nothing to do with animal welfare.

When I was a teenager I was an animal rights activist. I have been a vegetarian since when I was seven years old I connected the beef slices on my plate with the pretty black and white Friesian cows in the fields around my house. Some days later, a cod boiling in a pot looked to me like a fish swimming for its life and burning to death.

Luckily, my father, although something of an aficionado himself, understood. In the 1940s he worked in a cattle slaughterhouse for a very short time, and had also turned vegetarian due to the awful close up experience of all that death on his hands. My mother, a hoarder of stray cats, sparrows and any other animal to come our way, supported animal charities and this fuelled my passion to get involved, first with the more "harmless" varieties such as the Vegan Society but quickly I moved on to direct action with League Against Cruel Sports and ALF. By the time I was eighteen I was hunt sabotaging and photographing vivisection labs, even sometimes at the risk of losing my life, as indeed a couple of my colleagues did, in quite gruesome conditions which we won't dwell on here.

But there was a nagging feeling about one of the issues. A leaflet on the stall I helped run in Cambridge's King's Parade, the best hippy-student ratio road in the university quarter, was a leaflet calling for signatures against bullfighting. A black and white photo of the wall of a bullring, and a graphic of red blood across it. In big white letters, "Ban Bullfighting Now!" I read the text. "We the undersigned call for the ban of this cruel blood sport." There was a space for name, address, telephone number and signature which could be posted off to an address in Spain. (To this day I imagine a bullfighting organisation somewhere, with dusty old boxes full of these signed forms; a couple of old Spanish guys scratching their heads puzzling over their purpose, joking about where they keep coming from, and why they are in English, which they cannot read.)

But what the hell was bullfighting? I had no clue. I must have signed the petition about eighty times for "good luck". I saw it like I saw fox hunting; the mindless, drunken hobby of the upper classes in England, but with a bull. There was talk about how Spaniards threw donkeys from churches, and how bullfighting was dying out and only a few old people went. There seemed to be nobody who had been to a bullfight, and certainly no one I knew could explain what the bullfighter did, or why they killed the bull.

But over the period of the next fifteen years I probably signed about another fifty petitions such as this one without as much as looking up actually what takes places and why. It wasn't important to me. It was a fundamentally unacceptable activity: the killing of an animal for fun. This is the view of even the most media literate, worldly and intelligent people in the United Kingdom. We just don't get to see it in the media.

As for Catalonia? I asked around twenty well-read and well-heeled associates about Catalonia. Nobody I know, out of doctors, psychologists, teachers, musicians and writers knew where it was. People obviously knew Barcelona, but even people who had been to Barcelona, even frequently, had not noticed the speaking of Catalan, although some thought Catalan was "another type of Spanish". Many thought their own Spanish non-existent anyway, the classic "Doss servaysas pur favur"* being the only attempt. Lucky for them, a lot of people in Catalonia speak *Castellano* and Catalan as well as English and French in Barcelona.

Nobody I asked knew there was a separate parliament, and certainly nobody saw Catalonia as a separate country. If this is the information that the most savvy UK citizens have, it seems safe to assume that the less aware would have even less information about bullfighting in Catalonia.

So in July 2010, as one of the self-declared English ignoramuses (often called a *guiri* by the Spanish, who are well used to this breed of useless and rather obtuse Brits), when bullfighting was voted out in Catalonia, I took my father's mention of Orson Welles, Hemingway and Ordóñez the matador and searched my local library. I went to Ronda, one of the most famous bullfighting towns in Spain and pored over museum exhibits. By the time I finished my research, I was bursting with anticipation. Why did Catalonia ban bullfighting in the middle of an economic crisis, with nearly 30% of the population unemployed, and furthermore, offer monetary compensation to those affected? How can you relegate bullfighting to the history books when it has such a bright future in all Latin countries, and most recently France? What about the Southern Catalan tradition of the running of bulls, the correfoc and the correbous, where bulls are chased in the streets with horns ablaze with flames or fireworks for any drunken reveller to taunt it to death with any object he likes? Why was that wildly more frequent and popular activity not banned if the reason bullfighting was banned was animal welfare?

I had a year in Spain in which I could afford to travel in my tiny beat up car with my slightly out of date TV camera and make a film, in English and Spanish, to discover as much as I could about the Catalan situation and how it would affect the rest of the bullfighting world. I would go to bullfights. I would live and breathe the industry, spending days on bull farms, mingling with toreros, taurine clubs and society gatherings. I would also go and needle the politicians involved in the vote, and ask why they felt it was important for Catalonia, and for Humanity in the twenty first century. I wanted to understand what it meant to be Catalan, and why it was different to being Spanish. I would wax lyrical with Brits who write about Spain and the bullfight, and I would meet those who campaign against bullfighting and for animal rights, and those that campaign for Catalan rights. I would even visit and watch slaughterhouse activities, so that I could compare the life of the fighting bull to the life of the beef calf (To say bull here would be to suggest that a beef animal lives long enough to be considered an adult. They do not) which made me scream in the night and cry for hours. I would interview one of the most famous matadors in the world, and then one of the most knowledgeable, along with those as young as three years old who hope to be toreros in the future.

And when I came to edit the film, I found it impossible; because of the amazing contributions I had being so rich, so fruitful, so long! Yes, I had taped twenty one hours of footage and nearly all was useable. All was valuable. So I felt that this book would mean the intrepid viewer could also read the entire, untouched interviews also.

So, you may ask, what is my opinion now? I became vegan. The meat industry has a little sister, the dairy industry. This involves the slaughter of calves for meat, ripped from their distraught mothers, and chicks ground down still alive for the feed of their egg laying mothers.

This for me is absolutely unacceptable, and as Equanimal say, slaughter occurs in holocaustic conditions at a rate of 3000 animals a second. There is no respect for any animal killed for meat; in fact, according to some sources abuse by slaughterhouse workers is rife, including assault, torment and even rape. For me, my experience with modern halal methods was worse; a huge metal torture chamber slices the animal's throat back to the spinal cord (hence the animal can still feel and think) before leaving it to writhe around in its own blood for up to half an hour until death comes. There is no religious, sacred ritual here; just a tape of prayers playing on a bloodstained stereo to tick boxes. No, in the twenty first century we butcher animals with less respect than a thousand years ago. How "modern"! **

Bullfighting itself remains an enigma for me. Although I feel I can understand the point of the bullfight, I have not seen enough *corridas de toros* to have any right to declare any deep knowledge of the subject. But I do get it. My first bullfight shook me, then horrified me, then bored me. But I found myself thinking about every graceful movement, every glint of sun, every handsome face, every line that had thrilled me, against that pull of the belief system I thought I had set in stone for myself.

I did not watch the kill; in fact I filmed these moments with my eye to the camera but with my eye firmly shut. You can see in the film I was literally shaken by the experience when the sword goes in. I found out later talking to a well-known *aficionada* who has spent over fifty years travelling the world going to corridas, that she still shuts her eyes in defence of her love of animals.

The Bull and The Ban

But I forced myself to watch the next time. There was for me no meaning to this bull's life if I was going to be so disrespectful as to deny the moment of his passing in my experience. Society disrespects every animal it kills, every person it condemns by not watching. I felt it was important to honour the life of this creature, because, as Rafael at Equanimal says, it is a difficult thing to kill a bull, and for this, to my mind, its death needed to be experienced.

We humans hunger for the knowledge of death. Happy to watch murder mysteries and acted out shootings, dramatic rapes and staged horrors; TV studios now spend a fortune on prosthetics that imitate dead bodies so exactly that we now, ironically, judge if we enjoy a show based on the quality of its "gritty realism". Recently a man's death from illness was televised to high ratings. We look at photos of dead or starving children on a daily basis while eating our lunch. Galleries love to sell posters of war and its victims such as the famous Út photo of Kim Phúc running from a napalm attack in Vietnam while Hollywood churns out Nazi films to accolades every year. Mass murderers gain cult status and become sex symbols. It's meant to mean something, but what? We deny ourselves that reality first hand because we find it too raw, and yet happily reconstruct it as false instruments to satisfy some part of our psyche that knows we must die. Maybe watching the bull pass from this life to the next, in a surprisingly *gentle* kill in the bullring, is an ancient and civilised way of living with that always looming thought of death.

Or maybe, as the inheritors of the earth, bullfighting can remind us to take responsibility for the difference between humans and animals. We are man, they are beast. That is our luxury. We get to choose. Animals rely on humans and are part of our world, not the other way round. Perhaps if we keep trying to become "more civilised", a phrase that has become synonymous, wrongly, with "better" in today's world, we will lose the part of us that reminds us that we have that responsibility, that respect, that honour; to control our destiny.

As for cruelty, I certainly don't feel bullfighting is cruel by accident, or that those that support it have, in their deep, intelligent understanding and knowledge of everything taurine, have somehow not noticed the cruelty; a ludicrously patronising concept but one that many detractors hold. It's more straightforward to me. When you go to a bullfight you have bought in to that cruelty. You know it will come. Even if the bull is not killed in the ring, it will be steaks by dinnertime, because a bull, once fought by man, is rendered 'used' and cannot be re-used, in case he has learnt what the still figure next to the moving cape really is. Bulls learn fast; they have been bred from the smartest, most sensitive, fierce, brave and impatient of their herd, (the almost untranslatable word *trapio* is used to describe this quality in breeding) over centuries. So don't go thinking a bloodless bullfight is a morally superior one, if the moral system you hold dear is concerned with the death of an animal you paid to see taunted in a ring. It is by definition, a ritual between man and beast, and one may die, one may escape death. It is, during the last third, literally a flat playing field.

The Bull and The Ban

Bullfighting in Catalonia remains something less easy for me to have an opinion on. I am not Catalan, it is not my birthright. I will never know how it feels to be Catalan and the question about whether Catalan identity as a whole is compromised or enforced by this ban seems to depend on who I am speaking to at the time.

Since this ban, despite Mexico and Ecuador's *anti-taurino* activity, several cities in France, Spain and South America have protected bullfighting as Cultural Patrimony, and furthermore, since filming, Marilén Barceló Verea has led the way with her organisation in Catalonia to overturn the ban. At the time of writing they had achieved 600,000 signatures. So, ironically, as Jason Webster says, the act of banning the bullfight in Catalonia has indeed brought those off the fence and into the arena, setting back any attempt to see the end of the bullfight by several years.

So I feel I can only do what any worthy documentary filmmaker can do, which is to lay out the facts, and present to you the most inspiring moments I experienced during my fascinating time with the bulls.

*Dos cervezas por favor/Two beers please. In Spanish, the "v" is pronounced as a soft "b", the "z" as "th`" and the "o" as a short sound. Hence the jollity most Spanish waiters get from the pronunciation of the common English cry for lager.

**Anyone doubting this information, please watch "El Rito", a short film by Inaki showing Halal slaughterhouse footage, presented without comment, or visit the Mercy For Animals website for some undercover beef

slaughterhouse footage. I dare you to eat a steak after watching it.

The Law

PROPOSED MODIFICATION OF ARTICLE 6 OF THE UPDATED ANIMAL PROTECTION LAW 2/2008 PASSED ON THE 15TH OF APRIL 2008

MOTIVES FOR THE MODIFICATION

Catalonia pioneered an Animal Defence Law 1988. This avant-garde law, 3/1988, passed on the 4th of April 1988, among other things, prohibited the building of new bull-rings in Catalonia. The law has been modified and updated various times, always in favour of the rights of animals. An important modification was to prohibit children under 14 from going to bull-fights, as the witnessing of a violent act was seen to have a negative emotional influence on young people.

Another important addition to the law (22/2003 Animal Protection Law, 4th of July, 2003), declared that it considered that animals are psychologically as well as physically sensitive and it prohibited a number of spectacles and events where animals were caused suffering and were killed. So it would seem logical that, in the light of these modifications and additions, the law should include and protect bulls instead of excluding them. Objectively, bullfighting implies mistreatment and causes pain and suffering to the animals so the law should protect them.

Taking into account all these modifications, one sees that they form part of a process in the relationship between animals and humans. This process began from the totally anthropocentric point of view where animals were considered mere objects and continued to a substantiated point of view where, among other things, scientific evidence of the genetic similarity between species and of our parallel process of evolution, indicate that our laws must reflect this shift. Bulls (bos primigenius taurus) have a very similar nervous system to our own which means that we share many aspects of our neurological and emotional make-up.

Catalan society has, in general, accepted the evidence that bulls are capable of suffering and it has taken on board the shift in opinion which rejects mankind as having absolute rights over animals allowing them to treat animals with violence and aggression. This same shift in consciousness has meant that other countries, with long democratic histories, passed laws prohibiting events where animals were mistreated many years ago. . The combination of the growing concern among Catalan citizens to protect animals and the diminishing number of bull-fighting supporters plus the negative reaction that bull-fighting produces in visitors to our country and that fact that public money is spent to support these cruel events, clearly indicate the logical step which must now be taken: bull-fighting in all its legal forms must be abolished in Catalonia.

Therefore, in the light of the spirit of articles 148, and 149 of the Constitution and of articles 46, 116, 144 and 189 of the "Estatut d'Autonomia de Catalunya", the concerns of our Catalan society encourage us to formulate the following:

PROPOSED LAW

First Article

Letter "f" would be added to Part 1 of Article 6 of the updated text of the Animal Protection Law with the following text:

"f. Bull-fighting and events where bulls are killed, or wounded with the "sorts de la pica, banderilles i l'estoc" as well as any kind of event where bulls form part of a spectacle in bull-rings or anywhere else, except in the case of the events referred to in letter b) in Part 2 of Article 6.

Second Article

Letter "a" would be removed from the Part 2 of Article 6.

Additional arrangements

First. The Catalan Government will calculate an economic compensation to be given to those entities affected by the passing of this law; this compensation will be given within 6 months and will follow the usual legal procedure in such cases with petitions by those affected.

Second. The economic effects of this law will be accounted for in the budget of the following financial period.

The Bull and The Ban

Surrender of rights

Any ordinances or by-laws or rights which contradict this law or are incompatible with the contents of this law will be overridden or surrendered.

Final arrangement

This law will become operative on the day following its publication in the "Diari Oficial de la Generalitat de Catalunya".

The Ban

"And the results..."

July 28, 2010 - Catalan Parliament votes to ban bullfighting in Catalonia. Matador Serafin Marin looks upset as others celebrate. He is however, destined to fight the last bull in Catalonia a year later in Barcelona.

Alfred Bosch

Barcelona. It's three days after the last ever bullfight, and the mood in businesses around the plaza is sombre. Some shops display petitions to overturn the ban, while a bar owner tells me her business as a taurine restaurant is over. She has photos of all kinds of patrons, including Manolete the famous bullfighter, on her wall. I meet the wonderfully cheery Alfred Bosch, an award-winning Catalan author and academic, by La Monumental, the premium bullring in Barcelona. He is at the time waiting to see if he gets voted in as the leader of a coalition list with three leftist parties, Ezquerra Republicana de Catalunya, Reagrupament and Catalunya Sí. A few months later he is elected. I want to know more about Catalan separatism and how Catalonia is a separate country to Spain for many Catalans as well as his own experience of bullfighting.

So can you explain about Catalonia's current situation in terms of being a country?

Well, Catalonia is in fact a country, a different country from Spain. It's in the same state, it belongs to the same state, it's a little bit like Scotland and Wales, it's not just a province or region of this country named Spain, it's a whole different country with its own language and its own parliament and its own government, although right now it belongs to the Spanish state, and it's under Spanish rule.

So what makes it its own official country?

Well, of course it's very similar to what you can see and you can experience in Scotland for instance, lots of people here want independence, there's also many people who don't. So whenever there's a majority of people who want to become a separate country from Spain, probably there will be a vote and depending on the outcome on that vote, Catalonia will become a separate state with representation in the United Nations and diplomatic states all over the world. It really depends on the people and also on whether the Spanish government will allow the people to vote or not. We'll see if that happens, we'll see how it goes over.

OK, so tell me a bit about yourself and your work.

I'm basically a writer, and an academic, so I've been involved in civil movements related with asking for the vote, so that the Catalans can vote about their political status, and about their independence.

So if you can tell me — we are standing here outside La Monumental — why was it so important for Catalonia to ban bullfighting here?

Basically, sensibility; moreover the sensibility against animal mistreatment and for the rights of animals; so there was a movement, a popular movement asking for signatures so a law can be passed against mistreatment of animals in bullfighting. But this was moved by an independent NGO, nothing to do with party politics, but it was submitted to the Catalan Parliament which is the Parliament of Catalonia, it's an autonomous parliament within Spain. And this parliament, which is in its own area, decided that yes, there was a vote, and the vote was that bullfighting will be outlawed within Catalonia, but this doesn't apply to the rest of Spain. There's only one other area within Spain that also banned bullfighting and that's the Canary Islands. The only two areas within the Spanish state, on this Spanish monarchy, where bullfighting is not allowed.

Why do you think it was that bullfighting is banned but they have allowed fiesta bulls to continue, if it was about animal mistreatment, because the fiesta bull activities are considered to be much more cruel than the bullfighting?

The main notion here was a moral notion, that the big problem is turning the death or the killing of an animal into a show; there are other bull festivals all over the Mediterranean and it's very popular, but the killing of the animal is not like a public show. You can compare it in a way, humanising the process, you can compare it with public executions which took place until the end of the nineteenth, beginning of the twentieth century, public executions were held in the open, young kids could go and watch it. Of course, this evolved, sensibility changes, and this was stopped, at a certain period in time it was stopped because people considered it was immoral. It's very similar to that, the same way that some things were accepted, were considered morally right decades ago, centuries ago, burning people; some things now are considered unacceptable in the public eye. This doesn't mean – like stopping public execution doesn't mean stopping executions – stopping bullfighting and the show doesn't mean stopping the killing of animals, because among other things we eat meat and steaks which come from where they come, we don't just invent them; they come from animals. These animals have to be butchered and killed, but not as a public show.

And do you think that there is any truth in this; it was said that maybe bullfighting is going to be banned because it was an icon of Spain and the Catalan idea of becoming a country on its own, therefore rejecting that icon of Spain. Do you think it could be to do with that more than to do with the animal cruelty issue?

My impression is that Catalan nationalism or separatism is not anti-Spanish, it's pro-Catalan, and of course there's a struggle for Catalan rights, the right for holding a referendum, and people voting whether they want to separate or not from Spain; it's a question of democracy and rights, but it's not anti-Spanish in any way. I think the question here is whether Spanish power and the Spanish dictatorship in the Franco's years, the years of military dictatorship, really did a good job turning the fiesta into the national fiesta. I remember as a kid during the military dictatorship in Franco's years watching every Sunday afternoon, there was only one channel, one broadcaster for Spanish television, and we were like...if I wanted to watch television I had to see bullfighting going on and on all Sunday afternoon, and all these matadors killing one bull, two bulls, three bulls, four bulls... as a kid, watching this as a kid, this was like the symbol of Spain, of macho Spain, of military Spain, that was... the memory we have of that is a bit aggressive, a bit traumatic. So yes, there's a connection in the essence that this more aggressive, expensive sort of macho chauvinism in Spain was forced on us as kids and there is remembrance of that. It has not so much to do with Catalan independence or Catalan pride as it has to do with Spanish nationalism being forced in this way.

So, just going back briefly to the correbous question: why do you think that that has been left out of that ban? If we do take it as a representation of that time in Spain, why do you think it hasn't been put into place to be banned in the same way as bullfighting was? What is that difference, if you can tell me about that.

Well, parading with bulls, playing with bulls, even harassing of bulls on the streets which is very common in many places, has not been banned because the bull is not killed. The killing of the bull, which may happen later in the slaughterhouse, is not turned into a public show. And that is a critical thing, so that's where the buck has stopped right now. What would happen in the future? Well, maybe this campaign goes on and finally harassing of bulls in general will stop, or playing around with bulls stops. I don't know, it could happen, but the pressure is on and it could be anywhere along the line. Right now it has stopped at a very, very critical and important point, which is the killing, the public killing of the bull; turning it into a show.

So the actual building behind us is Barcelona's bullring, La Monumental. Could you tell me what you know about the recent history of this and what you've heard about what may happen to the building?

In fact, I don't know... I can't tell you very much about what goes on inside the bullring because I've never been in bullfighting, you know, to a bullfighting show. I don't have any friends that I can remember that have been inside; this has been basically a show, a subsidised show for tourists. And some followers, which are clearly a minority in this area, in Catalonia.

Regarding the building itself, there's a private owner so I guess he'll do whatever he wants to do with this building! The council as far as I know, doesn't have any plans for this, for buying the place, it's a very expensive building to buy because it's centrally located, so I have no idea, I don't know what would happen. I think the building itself could be preserved, in fact we have another bullring on the other side of town which has been preserved, or at least the outside has been preserved, and inside we've got like a commercial centre, which is nice, so something like that could happen. I think that the architecture by itself is alright, I mean, I like it personally, I have nothing against the building.

Do you think that there is any connection between religion and bullfighting in the sense that it could be something that is old fashioned and maybe has been rejected by Catalan people as well, because if you compare, say Barcelona to somewhere like Seville which is extremely religious and extremely fond of bullfighting, I mean, I can't go anywhere without seeing references. Do you think there's some connection there to modern times? Away from that kind of religious theme that you get running through with death?

I don't. Personally I don't see how you can relate Christian ethics with the torturing and killing of animals as a part of a show. Personally I don't see the connection.

The Bull and The Ban

When we went to Seville, we interviewed a lot of deeply religious people that really like bullfighting and they were saying animals have no souls, so therefore it's not a sin to kill the animal, what would you say about that?

I don't know if bulls have souls or not, I'm not even sure that people have souls! I don't know, but wouldn't that be a little far-fetched? My impression is that torturing people or animals is something which simply doesn't go into religious ethics. I think that's really trying to find, trying to justify something, which is very difficult to justify: Murder. I know one hundred and fifty years ago people were justifying slavery with similar terms, religious terms, saying the black people didn't have souls. I don't really care about souls, I care about suffering, and I think you shouldn't make people or animals suffer in an unfair excessive unnecessary way.

So do you think that when activists say that we shouldn't be doing anything to do with killing animals including eating meat, how would you make that line between eating meat and something like bullfighting, where is that line for you? What's the necessity there?

I think the line we should never cross is between things which are necessary and things which are unnecessary; making animals suffer, turning a killing into a show, is unnecessary, we don't need that, we can live without that. We can't really live without meat, we are carnivores, we are meat eaters, and that has to do with natural cycles, and that has to do with our diet, that has to do with something which is natural, for human beings and for many other animals.

The Bull and The Ban

Now that this ban has gone through successfully, how do you see that, how would you like to see that progressing across Spain as well as in Catalonia, would you like to see that progress?

Well, right now I am to go to the Spanish parliament, representing Catalonian parliament; if finally I go to Madrid, the parliament of Madrid, yes I would like to further that aim of that campaign, I would like bullfighting to go into history as part of the common history, I'm not rejecting it as part of the traditional culture but if you relegate it into history books rather than in public spaces...that's my idea, so anybody who wants to campaign further against mistreatment of animals or anybody who wants to ban the public killing of animals, if you want to get in contact with me, I'll try to help them, I'll try to help them in the Spanish parliament.

You are going forward to be a representative. Do you want to give people a bit more information about that?

I'm the leader of the list that Ezquerra Republicana de Catalunya – which is the Catalonian Republican Left – submits for the elections into the Spanish parliament, which are going be held in November 2011. Now, if I'm finally elected, I will be a member of the parliament; I'm going to further several causes but basically the cause of Catalan freedom, freedom to vote about anything we think we should democratically vote about, and also social justice because we are a leftist party, so we are also for social justice and especially fighting or struggling against human injustice in our country. That's basically my aim and also the defence of anything which may deserve fairness and be considered, which enters into our program, or ideals, and also will be fighting for that, and animal rights fit into that project so I'll be doing that as well.

Is there less respect for animals here than we would have in Britain, and why do you think that is?

Well, this is a Latin country, and that happens in most Latin countries, respecting the rights of animals is not as elaborate or evolved as you may find it in more Northern countries elsewhere in Europe, but that has also changed. I remember when I was a kid, dogs and cats were run over, and they were left on the street for the other cars to flatten them! I mean, that was quite a regular image when I was young, and these things no longer happen, so give us time, give us time, we are changing and maybe we won't reach the level of British decency but we will try!

Correbous & Correfoc

Fireworks on the bull's horns
while tail is pulled

Dressed up and paraded while carrying
a heavy cart and yoke

Tied to a truck while prodded with traffic cones

Horns set fire in the night streets,
taunted by drunken revellers

Antoni Strubell i Trueta

I meet the affable and erudite Toni Strubell in the grounds of the Catalan Parliament building, which flanks Barcelona's Parc de la Ciutadella. Toni Strubell is a linguist and author of the book, "What Catalans Want" as well as the coordinator for the Dignity Commission, an organisation which works to return documents, letters and photographs to their rightful Catalan owners after being seized by the Franco regime. The day we meet, the Spanish Air Force are preparing the way for the King of Spain's visit to Barcelona, so fighter jets constantly roar overhead, interrupting our filming; but poetically speaking, capturing the outrage that Toni, along with many Catalans, feels at the treatment given to Catalonia by the Spanish State in some respects. We choose a space by a beautiful statue dedicated to those lost in Franco's regime.

My name is Toni Strubell. I was born in Oxford fifty nine years ago, and I'm a member of parliament in the Catalan Parliament and a campaigner in favour of animal rights and against bullfighting.

Could you tell me about the history of Catalonia in the last sixty years, maybe from Franco onwards? So that people in Britain would understand why the independence is important.

Well, Catalonia is like Scotland. Catalonia is like the Scotland of Great Britain. On the agenda is the question of whether Catalonia can become an independent country in the next few years. This may be shocking to some people, but it's certainly I think shocking to us here in Catalonia to see the kind of treatment we get at the hands of the Spanish government in many fields. Just very recently the rights of Catalan speakers have been quite severely cut down in the sense that the use of our language as the language of education has been very much put in jeopardy recently.

At this particular moment in history, and we are in a very historic building, we are actually standing in the Catalan Parliament, the Catalan people are sort of divided at the moment about their future. There is a very wide scale feeling now that really there is no future in Spain. This may seem very dramatic to English people listening to me now, but the truth is that the agreements made that permitted the transition to democracy – the agreements made, and which led the Catalan people to reaching a commitment with the Spanish state – a lot of these agreements, a lot of these commitments have now been broken, and really the Catalan people feel very much threatened. Very often you hear Scottish people saying that they're going to get a better economic future if they're independent. Here there is a very real feeling that if the situation continues as today, economically we're really 'going to the dogs'. Catalonia is 'going to the dogs' at the moment. In one county near here alone 2,500 enterprises have closed down since 2007. There are now 700,000 people unemployed. This is really inexplicable from a logical point of view. This should be a rich country. It has been a rich country. And I think that Spanish misrule, and the fact that Spain has other plans for Catalonia means that our economy is really not sustainable in any guaranteed fashion.

I think one very good example is the question of the Mediterranean Corridor. It's really a case of, as you would say in English, 'cutting your nose off to spite your face'. Spanish economy has been based for years on the Mediterranean Corridor with exportation taking place from the Eastern strip of what is the Spanish state, and yet now it's very clear that the priority is to annul this Mediterranean Corridor in favour of a central Spanish Corridor. Now this will have a very serious effect on our economy, and so there's a lot of ill feeling here. So really, independence for Catalonia is one of the options of our future.

And I think more and more Catalans daily, even sort of very moderate Catalans, and even members of the socialist party that even ten years ago would have come nowhere near this kind of thought – even in mainstream newspapers like *Vanguardia*, which is now in Catalan as well. You find a steady trickle of Catalan intellectuals coming around to the general feeling that really within Spain there is no future. Again, this may sound dramatic but if you look at the figures, if you look at what's happening to our identity in many senses, and I know it's always polemical, controversial to talk about identity now but the truth is that now Catalan in school has been questioned by law courts in Spain, and this is leading to a situation in which more and more Catalans are coming around to favour independence.

Let's get to the subject of the ban. Could you tell me why bullfighting was banned in Catalonia, and how that relates to the economy and to the identity of Catalonia?

The Bull and The Ban

Well I'm not sure I really like the word 'ban' very much. I think that the Catalan people, as many European people, have come to the realisation that this is not on. You cannot make a public spectacle, at which children have been present up until very recently, and butcher animals in public. I think morally, ethically, it's something that goes against the sense of history.

One very often tends to think of 'Bullfighting = Spain'. The truth is that there was bullfighting throughout Europe and the same Wilberforce in England that banned the slave trade in England, also banned something else in England, which is bullfighting in England, which is something that not many people know about.

I think there's a sort of natural progression amongst the civilised nations of Europe to ban bullfighting, in other words, I think really, to recognise, to acknowledge the rights of animals and not to make a public spectacle of the agony of an animal.

Why has Catalonia been in the public eye? Why is all this scandal raised in Spain about Catalans wanting to accept the majority opinion of Catalans regarding the banning of bullfighting? In 1991, bullfighting was banned in Canary Islands and nobody made a song and dance about that. Nobody even noticed. But anything that happens in Catalonia, any rights that we demand here, any steps that are taken towards the home rule of the Catalan people, any steps that are taken towards making our sensitivity coincide with our legal status, is immediately fodder for the Madrid media who obviously come up in arms against really anything that the Catalan people ask for.

And I think that this is one of our major problems here. This is the truth, that anything that Catalans get around to wanting to change about their legal status is very much questioned from Spain.

I think that things that occur here, if they occurred in England they would be a question for the race relations board, which is an institution that in my time existed, I'm not sure if it still has that same name, but for example, things occur that would be unspeakable in England, like at big races, marathons held in the city of Madrid in which people taking part in a sporting activity actually carry big banners saying that – you know that thing that kids say 'the last one's an idiot' – well, 'the last one's a Catalan'. I mean, things like that may seem amusing but are a constant. One thing for example, we have just tried to renew our statute of autonomy, well, while we were trying to update our very legal structure, the Spanish bishops actually came out with a very aggressive campaign at the same time as the Partido Popular (A right wing political party) was collecting signatures against the rights of Catalans to do what they want within reason. The conference of Spanish bishops from their pulpits was engaged in whipping up a feeling against Catalonia, and actually the whole of the backdrop of the renovation of our statute, 2006/2007, was bishops coming on the television every other day saying that the unity of Spain is a moral quality. Well, can you imagine the Archbishop of Canterbury coming out and saying that all this Scottish business is immoral? Well, this is what we have to contend with in Catalonia, we have the church against us, we have a large part of the sporting community against us because Barcelona Football Club is unbeatable at this moment, but that also brings us to things that I think in England would be unheard of, that the cultivation of hate against the Catalonian people, I'm not exaggerating at all, would be something you would be finding in headlines every week in three or four major Spanish newspapers. So really it is a worrying question. I think the European Union would do very well to have a closer look at what is going on, because really a lot of the things going on here remind us to a certain extent – I don't want to exaggerate too much – of things that were going on in Yugoslavia in 1989/1990. Big Spanish radio programmes going on and on about the Catalans. Well, I'm very pleased to say that some European media have been on to this and I was very pleased to participate in a programme on Radio 1 in Holland about this very worrying question. I think Europe should be concerned about this.

The Catalans, we are made to live in a state where the death sentences passed by the Franco regime have not been annulled. Can you imagine in Germany, a situation in which death penalties applied by Hitler were not to have been annulled by the German democratic state after the War? This is the sort of thing that we have to contend with. Our president, the president of Catalonia, who was also the president of this Parliament, was executed in 1940. His death sentence is still standing. It has not been annulled. OK, some politicians came out and said that this sentence had been made illegitimate by the course of events. Well, any jury, any man or woman from the world of law will know that for something to be declared illegitimate means absolutely nothing. In the legal world, something is either legal or illegal. And those sentences are still standing, so to a certain extent, they are still legal. How do many Catalans feel about this? Well I think a lot of Catalans take a very dim view and I think the quality of democracy in Spain is something that has great shortcomings, and I think it's something that Europe obviously like Lord Nelson shows a blind eye to.

I've had occasion to explain to English people what actually goes on here, and the worst problem you have is actually one of credulity. A lot of people just think that you're inventing something. You know, the documents that were taken from Democrats by the Franco regime in 1938/1939 and taken to a police storehouse in Salamanca, they have still not been handed back to their legitimate owners in their entirety today. There are still things that occur that are very much a heritage of the dictatorship.

So the next thing we should talk about is bringing the subject together in those two threads that we were talking about with bullfighting and the identity and the cruelty angle. Obviously the pain of Franco's era is still prevalent in Catalonia, so would bullfighting be a reflection of that and do you think that's partly why people wanted it outlawed in Catalonia?

I think that may be part of the story, but Spanish history doesn't start with Franco. Unfortunately, the precedence goes back, much further back in history. There's one thing I'd like to say about the origin of bullfights in Catalonia. Those defending bullfights – there are still people that defend bullfights, even in Catalonia you find people that do defend this – they are always on about the fact that Catalonia has always had bullrings and this goes back so many years in history. Well, there are two things I'd like to say. The first things is that most of Europe had bullrings or bullfighting activities in the nineteenth century, so we don't have to go back that far to find most of Europe involved in this bloodbath. And the second thing I'd like to say is that the history of some bullrings in Catalonia for me is very stimulating to study because for example they will very often say that in the heart of the Pyrenees in the city of Olot, there is a bullring. Well, how can you find a more Catalan city than Olot? And there, sock in the middle, a bullring. Well, if you just look a little bit into the history, you find that that bullring was built by the garrison of the Spanish army in Olot. A big garrison for strategic reasons we can't go into here. And a lot of the bullrings built in Catalonia were actually built by the military, rather like this sound we're hearing now with the jets flying over. We can't get them out of our soup!

The presence of bullrings in Catalonia, it goes back years; I'm not saying that it doesn't, but it certainly has a lot to do with being grafted onto the Spanish political and military system. When a country is invaded, when a country is reduced to the laws of another country as occurred to Catalonia in 1714, where the great ancestors of the present king, the first Bourbon kings, built this building which was the arsenal of the Spanish Army. And all this park here is simply the firing range of the citadel of Barcelona, which was part of a fortress system built by the Spanish in Barcelona, which had many more cannon facing toward the population than they did toward the sea, so I think it's a unique case in Europe where the precedence of the military is not to defend the population against foreign invasion, but it's to ensure that the foreign invasion that there was, continues to succeed. This is the reality that we have around here. We are in the middle of what was a fortress. So I think these things are all relevant.

I'm sure that if Catalonia had been able to decide, bullrings would have been abandoned years ago. In 1901, the mayor of Barcelona opened up a very brave campaign to have bullfighting eliminated rather than banned, and obviously because of the pressure of Madrid this campaign was not possibly at that time. But I think that it's an important precedent. We have in 1901, where the mayor of Barcelona, in answer to the petition of the majority feeling of the Catalan people, attempted to get bullfighting eliminated, for humanitarian reasons, for animal rights reasons, and this was obviously not possible. I think that public opinion in Catalonia is that there's no doubt about it, I mean, here, the largest petition ever presented in the parliament was a petition in favour of the banning of bullfighting, so I think it's simply a democratic step that has been taken and I wouldn't dramatise things beyond that. There are questions of identity. There are also absolutely absurd arguments that are used by the pro bullfighting people. All of which I would now say have been ridiculised (sic) really.

Why is it that the correbous, the fiesta bull, the correfoc and all these kinds of things, why wasn't this all banned at the same time? Why was that a clause in Article 6?

This is a problem. And this is a problem that we are going to overcome. Bullfighting has been banned as from 1st

January, and yet the correbous, in which bulls tied to ropes and sometimes even with balls of fire attached to their horns are vexed, are baited, in the streets of some cities in the south and the very odd city in the north of Catalonia.

History is progressive. Anybody that wants to take a photograph of any development in history is going to have a sticky time. I think things develop. I would have liked that to have been in on the package, and I'd have liked the whole thing to have been suspended. And yet the idea that these correbous have more of a traditional leverage, or have more of a position, as regards to the tradition, it is probably true.

But I think that the fact that something is traditional or not is not the basic argument. Christians were killed in arenas, and that I'm sure was a very powerful Roman tradition. Well, the fact that it was a tradition does not justify it on ethical and moral grounds. It's all a question of the prism with which you see this. I'm very pleased to be able to say that the attempts to convince the European Parliament that bullfighting should be conserved have not gone beyond the first round.

On the same day that a concentration was held in favour of bullfighting in Brussels, three non-Spanish European members of Parliament attended the presentation of bullfighting. On that very same day, the anti-bullfighting lobby, with very discreet limited funds managed to organise a campaign that achieved the signatures and the support of hundreds of European members of parliament and thousands of civil servants in Brussels. And so I think that really the position that the defence of bullfighting now – it may be a heroic position but I think that the position is going to fall. It's going to fall because it's unsustainable in a modern and civilised Europe.

The fiesta bull – Do you know why they separated it out? I can understand what you've just said, but why was that decision made, to separate it? Was it economy, so that the bullfighting farms wouldn't just kind of have no money, what do you think it was?

The bulls that are used in the correbous have nothing to do with bullfighting farms, with the farms that produce the bulls for the bullfights. They are a completely different kind of bull, and very often they are actually cows. In fact, correbous, 'bous' means ox, it doesn't mean bull, it means the run of the oxen, so we're talking about something quite different.

Your question has no good answer. I'd love to be able to say "Well, a decision was made". I think politicians, we have our limitations everywhere, and I think you go step by step. I would have loved to have this whole show eliminated in one fell swoop. That was not possible and let's hope that within this mandate of the Catalan government, the next step will be taken. The question of votes is also – it's tragic but that's the truth – there is a lobby of pro-correbous population in the south, in the Ebra counties. I'm sure this has never really been measured, I'm sure there would be quite a shock if actually any kind of survey was conducted as there was in Andalusia. In Andalusia, the anti-bullfighting feeling is much stronger than the pro-bullfighting feeling. This is something that is very often hidden from the media. There are more people in Andalusia – which is the essence of bullfighting country – there are more people in Andalusia that secretly admire the decision made by the Catalans than one would think, and this is clear in some surveys that have been made. So it's not just the Catalans, I think it's civilised people anywhere.

In places like Andalusia, why do you think that people have such a problem with giving their opinion? Why are people scared to speak out about this?

I think this is true less and less. I think it's not so much a question of people being fearful about expressing their opinion. I think it's just a question of the cultivation of clichés. Here there are many, many clichés associated with the Franco regime, associated with so many aspects that we really need a fresh breath of democratic air to be dispelled across the table. I think it's just clichés. It's just a cliché. People think "Ah, Spain = Bullfighting" as they think "Catalonia = Spain". Well, Catalonia is something completely different! Catalonia is a country that wants its own European identity. We're a country that has always been... we're more part of France than we are part of Spain, mentally. I'm not saying that as a value judgement. That is where our history... that's where we come from. And that may also be a little bit of a contradiction because you may say 'Ah, well in France there's bullfighting'. The problem with bullfighting in France is that this question is sort of ignored by the State. It has been tolerated and has not been legally regulated until very, very recently. And there may be surprises I think in front. Really, what they do is turn a blind eye to the question of bullfighting, whereas here the Spanish make it into their sort of 'showcase'. The Catalans do not want to form part of this showcase, and I think one very surprising and shocking development of the last few months is that to spite the Catalans – I mean there is no other way of defining it than this – bullfighting, which up until now has formed part of the area of governance and the area of the Ministry of the Interior in Madrid has now been changed, and now forms part of the Ministry of Culture, which I think is an insult to the intelligence of Europeans.

It is just attempting to give the whole question, the barbaric nature of bullfighting, to try and give it another varnish, to try and sweep the decisions away, and I think one interesting question that we can ask is why was bullfighting in the ministry of interiors competences anyway? I think it just goes to show the mental structure of the defence of bullfighting as seen as something part of the State, part of the Ministry of Interior. Well now, of course, things have changed: Franco is no longer here to defend bullfighting, and so they have to bring it into a new showcase, which is the Ministry of Culture. Well, that's not going to work. That's not going to work in Europe and that hasn't worked for us Catalans.

"Rampova En Su Papamovil"   Courtesy Rampova

Rampova

Rampova was sent to prison aged fourteen during the Franco regime in Catalonia and the neighbouring region of Valencia, a province that also suffered terrible persecution under Franco. Rampova was arrested for being homosexual, which was a crime at that time. Rampova now exhibits paintings and performance art and gives interviews on local TV and in the national press, and works with performance and music groups on transgender issues through theatre, film, music and art. We meet in an art gallery that has shown his work in the centre of Valencia City. I bring ridiculous coloured meringue cake and everyone has a tiny piece. A film maker is filming me filming Rampova, making a documentary about his life. Rampova is pretty damn famous in this part of Spain, and known in a good few other countries too for his outspoken work. Although the reader may wonder why I included an interview with a gay drag queen in a book about the ban of bullfighting in Catalonia, I wanted to explore what it must have been like for those in society who were completely removed from the world of bullfighting when Franco was in power. I figured a gay transgender artist with strong opinions would probably do the trick. I was not disappointed. Rampova is a humble, wise and smart talker with the sort of face that masks a thousand stories. I wanted to know what it was like in a Franco-run prison for a person as individual as Rampova, and what bullfighting represents.

Can you give us a small biography about yourself... there will be lot of foreign people, American and British, that may not know about your work.

The Bull and The Ban

I've been three times in jail, twice in Valencia and this other one in which you give up living, in Barcelona. There you could find mobsters from Marseilles, all kind of dangerous people, even murderers; and bear in mind that was Spain during Franco era, when the *garrote vil* were used. A jailed man wouldn't ever see a woman and back then, being a kid with long hair was the best excuse for being raped. That determined your life forever, and then you didn't have the right to have a passport nor get exiled, not even the right to work, because jobs required a 'good conduct' certificate, and who did those certificates? The police, who had you in their black lists!

So most of us dedicated ourselves, those of us who "had art", between quotes, to showbusiness. I "had art", and I learnt a lot too; I met some people and together we founded a group called "Ploma 2" (Camp 2); we did music hall. Also we learnt dancing from Olga Poliakoff and switched onto cabaret because we wanted to make our art more 'critical' and then we 'criticised', we put on a socio-political satire where all kinds of critique fits. Obviously, and unfortunately, in the gay places we weren't welcome; however we were a success in other places. In the business, we were the only ones doing presentations in universities, the philology faculty, Valencia faculty, geography and history faculty, and then the last one in the Pedreguer faculty in 2004 doing, "Open the Door and Get Out of the Closet". Not so many drag queens can claim that and be proud of being in those places!

Do you think that bullfighting is rejected because of being bound, linked to "Franquismo"?

No, because bullfighting existed at least three hundred years ago. On the way to... I can't remember the name of the town, but on the way to Alicante, there's a bullring that is a masterpiece, with Arab vestiges; since then it existed. Anyhow, as Spain had two ephemeral republics, then Franco, the dictatorship of Primo de Rivera and a few absolutist monarchies, obviously people associate this to a black and savage Spain.

And about the gay community... what do you think about the men, the bullfighters using the "traje de luces"... as you said before the interview?

Well, I think there's a huge contradiction; there is a big contradiction because what they call traje de luces is in fact a glittering sequin dress, and if I were wearing that in the streets, not in the cities, but in the small towns, people would stone me! First they wear an outrageously glamorous costume: if I was to wear a bullfighter jacket and pants, and go to some small town's streets, especially those of the extreme right, it's not only that I may be stoned, but I can easily being killed!

Do you think there's something in common between the contrast in the Franco period, between the repression of the people and the exaltation of bullfighting?

Back then it was said that to make people stop thinking, mimicking ancient Rome, they used "Panem et Circenses", from Latin: Bread and Circus. The circus was the Holy Trilogy composed of football, bullfighting and the mandatory church. If you weren't going to church and you were a kid, you got punished for a week, what they use to call "No Recess".

When people consider bullfighting as art, what do you think? Do you think it can be considered as that? People say bullfighting can't be abolished because it's a tradition, a kind of art, what's your opinion about that?

Twelve years ago I said that if bullfighting is an art then cannibalism is the height of fine gastronomy!

The Bull and The Ban

La Monumental, Barcelona..

Matador Serafin Marin triumphs
with the last bull of the
last ever bullfight in Catalonia.

He is carried through the streets
of Barcelona carrying the
Catalan flag...

25 Sept 2011

Marilén Barceló Verea

The Bull and The Ban

Marilén Barceló Verea is a Barcelona psychologist who has written books with taurine and psychology themes. She is the daughter of Luis Barceló, the Catalan matador, and is campaigning with La Federación de Entidades Taurinas de Cataluña for the overturning of the bullfighting ban. I meet her at the Polo Real Club in the business district of Barcelona where she rides horses. Her friend speaks English and offers to conduct her own interview, which I then tape. So really this is the conversation of two friends who both adore bullfighting and want to show the problems for Catalan aficionados. Marilén is passionate about bullfighting, but also about her identity as a Catalan, and as a Spaniard. She is deeply concerned for the future of Catalonia in light of the ban.

What is your relationship with bullfighting?

Well, the truth is that as it comes, it starts; it's like a gene. I had the luck to have a father who has been, or still is, a bullfighter, because a bullfighter is always a bullfighter. And since I was a little girl the hobby has been part of my growth, in my evolution as a person. I did my PhD in psychology about the world of the bull, therefore, that interest in bullfighting allowed me to unify my vocation in psychology with the world of the bull. So now I'm in the Federación de Entidades Taurinas de Cataluña as vice-president, trying to make this ban not take effect next year (2012).

The ban hurt us a lot. I think Barcelona has always been a universal, plural and open city, and the ban affected us a lot, I think it goes beyond bullfighting; we are ignoring a basic principle all human beings have, which is freedom. Catalonia and Spain have always been the reflection of democracy; Spain, after the Civil War was the perfect example about how to live in a democracy, and now we are putting at risk important values, and Barcelona can't afford that luxury, neither Barcelona nor the central government should allow this ban to go ahead, as if it does I think Spain will become a dictatorship.

In the prohibition, there's a paragraph in Article 6 that differentiates between bull festivals that, if it's bullfighting in the street, activities are not forbidden. What do you think about Article 6?

Well, I think we are talking about hypocrisy, I mean, in Catalonia the ILP has been forbidden, previously approved by the "Parlament de Catalunya"; they also banned bullfighting, but not some other bull festivals, such as the correbous. Hypocrisy. The bull is always the same.

What is a correbous?

A correbous is a popular festival in Catalonia, in many different places in Catalonia, many towns, where the bulls are run. There is also the correfoc, which is a bull with the horns on fire, and those are actually not banned, as those generate several votes that many political parties wish and need to govern. Here there is the hypocrisy, the bull is the same, don't forget that the bull in the ring has a regulation. When we talk about the bull, we are not talking about a domestic animal, we are talking about a brave animal, an animal with the ability to charge, it's not as other animals like the lion, or a tiger that simply attacks, the brave bull charges, that's why it goes with true mettle, it goes to the capote, goes to the muleta, you place the capote, you place the muleta and the bull has the inertia to go for it; that is a brave animal, and in the bullring there is a regulation that takes care of the *toro bravo*, that makes sure all rounds are executed properly, and ensures the bull is in optimal condition to deal with it, so that about separating the bullfighting and the correbous is just more hypocrisy from the Catalan government.

Also in the bullfighting, as far as I know, there's a bull and a bullfighter, and the bull has the ability to be indultado, *or kill the bullfighter?**

Exactly.

While in the correbous and correfoc there is a bull against...200? 300?

A lot of people.

And what do those people do? Beat the bull between all the people, punish the bull, does the bull have any kind of defence in a correbous?

It's very different, and has nothing to do with it but I'll say it again: Hypocrisy, I mean, I don't know if I've been fortunate or unfortunate to be at both *comparecencias* taken in the Parlament de Catalunya defending bullfighting.

The Bull and The Ban

Explain a bit about the correbous, the fact the bull ends up jumping into the river as people kill it with sticks ....they are not professionals. But the ban is only for the regulated bullfights?

Regulated and maintained.

The ban is not for when the bulls are against many people...

No, the ban is not for the correbous or some other popular festivals.

And how does the bull finish up in those situations?

In all these there should be some rules, if you take care of the rules, everything should end well, and if you don't... I wouldn't like to know how those bulls finish up, I mean, I'm more of the opinion that, and I respect all opinions, having a set of rules in any popular festival where a brave bull is involved; just think about it, the *taurinos* love the bulls, we care about them, they spend five years at the farm; it's a lie whenever people say the bull is transported in poor conditions. The first person wanting the bull to arrive alright to the plaza is the farmer. The brave bull is a cult animal, it's an animal completely different to a dog, horse or cat, and then, any festival, either bullfighting or any other popular festival, what you have to look for is the integrity, and it has to be regulated. Probably that regulation must evolve too, as everything, but don't mix things that have nothing to do with each other. The bull's ban in Catalonia has nothing to do with the care or abuse of the bulls, absolutely nothing, it's just hypocrisy, and especially an attempt from the government that doesn't like any Spanish identity, on which I think they are wrong. Spain is Spain, we are all together, I said that at the beginning of the interview, after the Civil War, Spain was the best example of unity and any separatist attempt I think causes a lot of damage to the Catalans and all the Spanish people.

The toro bravo is a unique animal in nature, so if you don't know about it, to give your opinion about it is impossible. Apart from that, there's a lot of fear to talk about death. It was talked about in the Parlament de Catalunya to do a Portuguese bullfighting style, but hey, in the Portuguese bullfights the bull still dies in the plaza!** It's fine now, the hypocrisy we all have, isn't it? Whenever one sits down and eats, whenever one... there are other animals, I mean, don't be hypocrites, it's a ritual of life and death, it's a metaphor of the same life. And it's true that whenever the bull comes to the ring, apart from the bravery, apart from that innate ability to charge, it's a wonder seeing a bull charging, it has that nobility that makes the fighting bull father of other bulls. It's there, the nobility and greatness of the world of bulls, the evaluation of a unique animal, and whenever we talk about a brave bull we are talking about a whole ecosystem, at the farms, the toro bravo generates other animals, creates a very important ecosystem, for people to survive; therefore whenever the bullfighting festival is attacked, the human being is attacked.

What does the ban mean for the bull industry in Catalonia?

The Bull and The Ban

I think that what is happening in the world of the bull... Look at Ortega y Gasset, he smartly said, and I think he was one of the big masters, he said that whenever one goes to the bullring, one could see how the Spanish reality was, but I don't understand him. In an era where the economy is not in its best moment, in an era where public health has been touched and should never been touched in the way it was, in an era where there are people in the queue waiting for surgery, where health is being toyed with, the fact they think of a ban that will have an economic compensation, which has a lot of jobs, really, that's ridiculous, it goes against citizenship! I mean, how you can think of the bull industry, with all the jobs it generates? I mean, first it generates jobs, then generates other indirect jobs, culture, art, the textile jobs, apart from the tourism, there are a lot of businesses depending on the toro bravo industry. How a government can even think about suppressing all that business, and then what's even worse, an economic compensation, now? With the crisis we have, I'm right now, as a Catalan, feeling totally humiliated; the fact the priority last year in the Parlament de Catalunya was talking about bullfighting. Hey, you know how the economy goes in our country? What are we really doing? Where is it? The day after the ban, I woke up and I felt bad, because I grew up in freedom, and now I realise the city I love is not as it used to be; that hurts a lot.

Is it true that for Barcelona, the bullfight that happened this last weekend made the hotel prices triple, so Barcelona's revenue increased a lot?

That's the reality; if you see in a plaza, whenever the plaza is full up to the flag, as is commonly said in the bullfighting world, which generates expenses, doesn't it? Travelling, hotels, food, dinners, shopping — La Monumental was full, the fact is that there are some people who don't want to see the reality, but those numbers are obvious...

La Monumental has a capacity for 18 thousand people, who come to Barcelona...

And I wonder, how anyone can think that those 18 thousand people there have a problem with their mental faculties? In fact, something else that hurt me a lot, really a lot; those people against the bull festivals; because to me, anti-bullfighting, in this century, it's a bit ridiculous. They were insulting us, provoking us; how is a government allowing that? Isn't that banned? Then, respect it, why the continuous provoking? What do they want to achieve? An altercation?

Is there any ban on boxing in Barcelona?

As far as I know, no. And it's a sport also, and I respect it a lot.

And the people that go to a boxing show, they have people in front shouting, calling them assassins, and the government allows it?

It's allowed, there it is, I think, in boxing, I respect it a lot, it's not a sport I used to watch but it's a sport and I respect it as it is. But it's really that, what the Catalans

71

have suffered is something where you say, "It couldn't happen in my city", it's impossible, no? The insults, the provoking, no? Because I think the worst is that they like provoking you.

I think that Convergencia y Union, Mr Artur Mas, we have to reckon it's not easy for him what he's confronting, I mean, he got a government that was previously bankrupt, so his mission is not easy, maybe whenever there's a Spanish government, and let's hope it comes soon, the future Spanish president, the new Spanish government won't have it easy as all the problems will be inherited, people complain about cuts, but they were generated by the previous politicians. What doesn't make sense, with Mr Artur Mas and Convergencia y Union, which is a political party, we may agree or not about how he governs or about certain facts, but he's a politician that also made good for Catalonia in some other moments; he can't allow it, he can't.

Is it true that if the ban is reverted there's no need to get a cent of public money to pay anyone?

Of course, but I think it's incoherent that the bullring is prioritised. I think it is a private company, and as a private company it has the right to compensation; I'm not against it but it's not the right moment. Then, whenever it's not the right moment, something that generates income, they cut it and then have to compensate. It seems completely absurd that a business that used to generate income then suddenly is closed and they are compensated! Where are we? What kind of Spain are we? It's unrecognisable.

The Bull and The Ban

Do you think this ban was proposed because people identify the bullfighting as Spanish identity?

Yes, and it hurts me to say it, and what these nationalist parties are doing is not the mirror of Catalonia reality; here all the people speak Catalan and Castillian with absolutely normality; what happens is that here Catalan language is imposed, that is the problem. But the people, the Catalans – I love Catalan, whenever I speak Catalan, I think in Catalan and I love to speak Catalan; but languages are made for us to understand each other, so then for us to understand it is better to speak a language we all understand, full stop. And we should really speak many languages.

So they are really wrong, because in Catalonia there's an incredible bullfighting tradition from a long time ago; there's like an addiction to the bull, to that Spanish symbol. Because in fact, I wonder, let's be a bit ingenuous now at this point of the interview and let's think that they focused on the bull only as the animal, because as far as I know, the Osborne bull is not alive, and the Osborne bull has been eradicated from Catalonia. Then if the Osborne bull, which is a bull I like a lot but it's just cardboard – that bull, that whenever we arrive to a Spanish region we have the Osborne bull as a symbol, in Catalonia they have been removed. Why? Because they are synonymous with Spanish identity. So of course there are many attitudes that make us suspect the hypothesis that they are going against Spanish symbols.

You well know there's no second election round in Spain, but there are some parties that are elected and then they

73

don't exist, between the finalists only two are elected and then there are the elections, and sometimes there are some parties who don't have enough votes, but they are the ones who balance the "yes" or the "no" in certain circumstances...

When Mr Montilla was president of the Generalitat, it was then the ILP for the ban was approved; it was supported by Ezquerra Republicana de Catalunya; that was the price to govern. He didn't have enough courage to stop that ban, he didn't have enough courage because he wanted to stay in and get the support to continue governing. Seems absurd, but it happened here and also in other Spanish communities. I mean, it looks absurd; it's a fraud, when you vote for one party, for them to make a coalition with another party that has nothing to do with your ideals.

A party that has nothing to do with your ideals and represents like 3% or 4%, maybe 6% of the population...

Decides...

... Then that party is the one deciding everything?

It's like that! Like they used to say, many times, that the minority parties have the key. I mean, they decide what would happen or not, and that's the price of power; all people like power, all people like to govern.

Then there are politicians that have 40%, or 45% of the votes, and their electorate, as is the case in the Socialist party... it's obviously, and objectively, immigrants coming from many different places of Spain, and bullfighting fans, their representatives were sold for a few votes to other people that are separatist?

It's like that; you see the party supporting bullfighting the most is the Partido Popular with Mr Mariano Rajoy as the main secretary, especially in Catalonia, with politicians such as Alicia Sánchez Camacho, Alberto Fernández, Rafael Luna; they've been consistent. I mean, independent of the political ideals anyone may have, there's a reality. The world of the bull felt supported by that party, as well the Spanish Partido Popular as the Catalan Partido Popular; they always were consistent, and nobody should forget that the Partido Popular defends not only the bullfighting festival but freedom, because even inside that party there are some people who have never come to a bullring but they respect the freedom. I'm really surprised about other kinds of parties, always proud of being progressive, being open, having the freedom as a flag, but allowed this ban, and here the socialist party has not been noble; it was another reflection or commentary on Ortega's politics in Spain.

In Catalonia, do you think it was wanted to identify the bull with Spain in an insistent way?

Yes.

...While the bull is a universal animal, while the bull and bullfights happen in Portugal, Colombia, Mexico, Venezuela, millions of people are tied to this culture in many countries; many different ways of thinking, and

75

here it was insisted that the bull is only in Spain, while obviously it's a universal animal...

Yes, you see, that's what is beautiful; the magic the bullring has to unify all. They have been wanting to sell the bull as belonging to an old Spain, a bad Spain, but that's a lie. The bullring, that wonder it has is that it unifies, two fans with different political ideologies, with different football teams, they are united because the magic that happens in the ring and with that word saying "Ole", that has no translation that anyone knows. Then bullfighting unifies, and as far as I know, there was never a problem, you can go to a football match and you can see a fight sometimes; that doesn't happen in a bullring. And I think the bullfighting ban damages the values, through the bull festivals you can learn a lot: tradition, courage, constancy, responsibility, effort; whenever you fall in love with what happens in the ring, whenever someone got shocked with that magic between the bullfighter and the bull, that one between life and death, between the effort, the sacrifice, responsibility, sensitivity; there's a set of values that makes whoever watch the bullfight feel it. The world of the bull has a set of values that if we maybe appreciate them more, will make us grow as human beings.

Is it true that in a bullring, between the bull and the bullfighter, it must be the only place where there are no lies? As the bull is in front of the bullfighter?

It is like that, I mean, whatever happens in the plaza is true, there's no trials. A bullfighter close to me, my father, who taught me the most; one day he said very appropriately, "In bullfighting, the bullfighter needs to know everything, but nothing is programmed", because it's like that; they need to get all the technical knowledge, as bullfighting requires a technique, but once you get a bull in a ring you can think it will go one way or another; you have seen many, but you've got everything, the bull in front; there are no pauses, no recordings, no rectifications, nothing. There is no "erase, save and archive". Everything is real, and exposing the most important thing: your life! But not only the physical life, because I think while facing the bull I wouldn't even know how to handle the capote. I would think of my physical integrity, but they don't, they think of responsibility, the fear of failure. A bullfighter, imagine: we all work, but imagine that work being continuous, and also exposed to the public. Oh, there are a lot of values there.

Is it true that a bullfighter always tries to kill the bull in the first attempt so he doesn't suffer, as the bullfighter will never forget it, as the bullfighter loves the bull? Is it true that whenever the bullfighter has two or three attempts, the 18 thousand people jeer him and shout him to make him feel the shame of making the bull suffer? A fan never wants the bull to suffer?

The bullring has a president that regulates all, and also you have the fans, here you have the democracy. Never as the votes now. A handkerchief asks for an ear, insisting also the president allows the second one. It is true, I have to say because I'm very objective, well, subjective as I love the bull festival, and I feel no shame at all saying that I grew up loving the bull festival, that I still love it; you can forbid me, as a Catalan, to go to a bullring, but you can never forbid me my feelings, nobody can take out my *toro* feeling, that's something that is for me, no politician can remove it.

I also think there are a few rounds, as in the supreme round, that after trying it (the kill) twice, to try it for a third time... it's something that has to be approached in a different way. Because I think things have to evolve, and the taurinos are sometimes guilty of not evolving at the rhythm of society, and that's a fact we have to realise, that we'll have to evolve, but also realise there are some warnings, like when the round becomes too long, and the bull comes inside...

If there's a regulation that doesn't allow too many attempts to kill the bull, once there are a determined number of attempts, it can be stopped and the bull is put out of its misery, so it doesn't suffer.

A bull, up to arriving to the plaza, from the farm, is selected between hundreds, a bull once it arrives to the plaza, even when is selected, is checked by a vet to verify it's OK and that nobody touched it, that it's healthy, without scratches. How then you can say tauromaquia *is cruel when the bull is treated like a king until it enters into the plaza, then it has its chance, even its chance to be pardoned and survive, then how you can say the tauromaquia is cruel?*

Ignorance, here you have the ignorance, it was said by Poper that the fruit of ignorance is to not want to acquire knowledge.

The Bull and The Ban

With the bull, there's a vet team, the bull has a selection in the farms, the bull arrives alone in its own transport, the bull is weighed to check it didn't lose weight during the travel; the bull is cared for, the bull is checked by a vet. In fact, once the bull goes out, there are many rounds that will determine the continuation, I mean, the bull is the most cared for animal; whenever people say the bulls were without drinking water in the farm, that it has been drugged, what do they know? They have no idea that never happens, it's impossible, because of the farmer, first, because the bull has some expenses, but even further, the farmers live for the brave bull, the taurinos, we love the nature. You will see a taurino with a fly and they will open the window to let it go, they never kill it, that is a taurino, you know, I've lived that at home, I had animals my entire life, dogs, horses, there's a unique love with animals.

You think there's a confusion between what is tauromaquia, that it's a revealed and regulated art, with a bull, farms, vets and so on, and the barbarism that is allowed in some towns where people take, not a bull but a heifer that has no value, and then they put that on it? Is that tauromaquia for you?

Not for me, I'm very sorry as I know this will be an answer that may hurt some susceptibilities but now I'm not answering as a vice president of the federation, I'm answering as Marilén Barceló. Personally this kind of festival doesn't make me feel anything.

But is that tauromaquia?

The Bull and The Ban

Not for me, not for Marilén Barceló, I like the bull in a bullring with rules, maximum care, and also the bullfighter at his best, showing the bull at its best, that's what the best bullfighters have. Here the bullfighter is able to show the bull at its best, as for example Enrique Ponce, there are many good bullfighters, but this one was off the top of my head, he's one of the big ones that has that sensitivity to make it look easy, but it's not, to show the bull at its best always.

Then why is it so important for the bullfighting to continue in Barcelona?

Do you think that now the ban is allowed, we may have governments that may forbid any other thing they think of while on the other hand people are allowed to smoke drugs on the streets, allowed to steal, and as they are minor thefts, people are not jailed, and many other things that cause damage to citizenship?

Catalonia and Catalan politics had a step back in its history. I think we made a reverse step, we had a step back, I mean, it's very hard to say, me saying those words, I think when I was a kid I never thought that I would say that Catalonia did a step back in its democratic history, but yes gentlemen, it has been lost... the politicians, if they ever have to respect something it's freedom, I thought that's what makes them politicians, isn't it? Freedom and democracy, yes. Spain did a step back. Catalonia did it but the Spanish government allowed it. I think the damage done to us is beyond repair.

The government, the state, the communities, the Generalitat, do they spend a cent from their pockets for the bulls?

Nothing, absolutely nothing, they finance themselves; there are, obviously, the typical grants for the farms, but it's a private company managed by itself, and no Catalan granted any bull festival.

Is agriculture financed in Europe?

Of course.

Is it more or less 30% of the European community budget for agriculture?

There, you are saying it.

What do you think about the universality of the bulls outside Spain and Catalonia, for example, when the Portuguese, even the Portuguese travelled to Colombia, then they come to Spain and they show their own customs, they feel proud of bullfighting their way, they have their tradition on top. The Spanish wear a short costume; the Portuguese have a jacket, all the traditions involved in many countries, the diversity that the bull unifies, in the entire Latin America, the whole Spain, Portugal...

That it has great value; the universality, that also the fiesta has been conveyed; it's a tradition that has been happening, has evolved, and as in traditions, all adds a little grain of sand. That is the most beautiful, that's the most magical, that one can get excited with a bullfighter from Colombia as well as a bullfighter from Madrid, as with a Catalan one, as with a Mexican bullfighter, that the magic we have, that's the magic of the culture, of the tradition, that it was able to survive against time, a show of a big tradition uniting all the people. In fact I'm plenty convinced that the Catalan that doesn't go to a bull festival, even when they don't come, won't ever forbid it, because Catalonia has always been a good example of freedom and respect.

What do you think of the fact there is another new rule, forbidding the kids to go to the bullrings, while kids on the street can see people smoking drugs and that's absolutely legal?

Well, I think that's barbaric, there's also a study done by the "Defensor del Menor", in the community of Madrid, endorsing the fact the kids going to the bullfights didn't cause any problems. Here, here's a good example! (She points to herself)

Do you think it's educational that kids can see people smoking marijuana and hashish on the streets?

Of course not, and I see it coming, in fact, I'll tell you something, I came to the bullring when I was a kid and anyone can analyse me and check that I have all my mental faculties, and my job is a job that I think helps people, I'm a psychologist, I help people with their emotional world, and probably that sensitivity I have for the problems of people may teach me a lot in the world of bulls. I can tell you, I think there were like 19 thousand people the other day in the Monumental, and I think we were all in good mental health. Now if they want they can analyse us, because people have told me I'm an assassin, they have insulted me, saying I'm an abuser; first analyse me, meet me and then judge me.

Before the ban, it was forbidden that kids younger than 14 years old went to the bullrings, because they could be mentally affected, but it's not forbidden for kids to go to the zoo, where the animals are jailed, animals that never lived in freedom; they were born in the zoo and will die in the zoo, while the brave bull was born in freedom on the farm, and dies free as it has the chance of being pardoned, how it can be possible to have zoos in all the cities in the world?

How can it be possible that kids can go to the zoo to see all kinds of animals and their behaviour when in a zoo, an animal, a lion, can't show their behaviour – is that healthy, while it's mentally bad to see a bull in freedom?

Here you have one of the biggest contradictions of our Catalan government, because Mr Portavella was always against bullfighting, when he was managing the Barcelona zoo, he had our "Copito de Nieve" (Snowflake the albino gorilla later euthanised after thousands paid to say goodbye) on its last days, exhibiting it to the public. So then, there you have the big contradiction, because I know a bit about animals, and when an animal is close to death, it wants to be with the people who take care of it, not totally exposed to the public, where many souvenirs were sold to promote the last goodbye to "Copito de Nieve". There you have it, in fact, many years ago a bull was sent to the Barcelona zoo, the bull tried it, I think it was in Barcelona or some other zoo, I can't remember, the bull didn't survive, he couldn't live there. It's a brave animal, not an animal that can live in a zoo. These are the big contradictions in our government; the government banning the bullfight wasn't even able to respect the dignified death of "Copito de Nieve", or the zoo, or Catalonia.

We all know how people love things like shoes, belts, bags, leather purses, that are, in the end, from a cow, and it doesn't matter if they are from big brands, big fashion designers; we won't provide names for advertising. People eat meat: chicken, pheasant, fish and so on, all animals, to take care of all these animals is ecological, then it is fashion, it's cool, but why now public money has been spent on these campaigns where the fashion is going against the bull? Not the chickens, not the belts, not the bags, no, they are made of skin too, but only against the bull, is it because it identifies with Spain?

Well, I think there are two reasons, I mean, I'll also talk about the opinion they give you, it's a question I have, they don't understand the show, they can't understand that we go to a bullring to watch a show. It's an art, the expression of a feeling where the bull has the chance to express itself.

But they pay their money for the people...

No, I mean, that's what we've been talking about in the whole interview, the hypocrisy, I mean, now I've come and then I go against the bull, but I think all those politicians, in this case, from Convergencia y Union, when we chat with them, they gave us their favour, then they changed as there were a few open lists (not party set) for Catalonia's elections, and that was so...

Because of the fact there's no election system of two...

No, because the man who takes the decisions told them if they want to be in the lists they have to either abstain or vote against it, against the ILP. Then I think what really happened was hypocrisy, because I'm plenty convinced those politicians eat, dine on and wear animals. But of course it's very difficult to be coherent in this life, and what is coherent? Whenever one is coherent in thinking and action. But the coherence is missed a lot in the politician class, and if the coherence is not enough for people who govern us it's a risk.

Do you think politicians today, not only in Catalonia and Spain but the rest of Europe, if they leave politics would they be able to make a living from something else? And that's why they need that seat at any price?

Well, I think there are very good politicians, and some other ones not prepared, I mean, what I ask from a government is the capacity to rule, I mean, a health minister must be prepared, a defence minister must... feel the military part and must be prepared to exercise it. The problem comes when someone takes office and is not prepared to work the job, and obviously that person, if you place him in another job, won't get neither the purchasing power nor the privileges that certain ministers have.

Is it true that people who love tauromaquia, not the bull shows, but tauromaquia, love the bull and they don't want the bull to suffer?

Always I think taurinos are bull lovers, nature lovers, and we defend an animal completely different to any other animal. What is happening is that many people talk about the bull and they don't know about it and the ignorance makes them, sometimes, say absurd things.

Whenever you tried to explain what the bull means, have your views been heard? Or simply do they do what their image consultants and votes consultants told them?

They never wanted to listen to us, and at more than one opportunity the Federacion de Taurinos de Cataluña, and me personally, we offered to sit down with them and chat about the subject, but they never wanted it. They are more worried about the place they have on TV, their image, and those arguments that make no sense. Because I heard that they said the toro bravo was different... that the bull in the ring was different than the bull in the correbous, so just imagine, the great ignorance there!

So they don't distinguish between a chicken and a hake...

No, they don't distinguish what a bull is, no, no, they can't distinguish between a brave bull and a domestic animal, I mean, a cat is a cat, a horse is a horse. I've never seen in my life a dog charging, or my mare charging, then they don't distinguish the concept of an animal, there are domestic animals and brave animals, and they don't know the concept of bravery, they miss this point.

The German Shepherd is the same as the poodle? Both are dogs.

Both are dogs.

The bull in the bullring is the same animal as the bull in a correbous?

Of course, obviously from another farm, maybe with another trapio but well, there are some farms with some different trapios.

Do they both have 4 legs, 2 horns and a tail?

They are called bulls; you can say all are that! (Laughs)

Marilén's friend has had her name omitted. She was scared of reprisals from anti-taurinos, colleagues and others in Barcelona. She told us that Catalans are scared to speak out about bullfighting. In the taxi back from the interview, she asked the driver, "Do you like bullfighting?" He answered, "What am I allowed to say?"

*It is highly unlikely that a bull would be pardoned if he kills the matador, so this is probably not a fair measure of how the bull would survive. Normally, the Senior Sword would come into the ring and kill the bull in the normal manner once the gored matador is carried from the ring. Indultado bulls act "nobly" and give a good show until the

last minutes of the faena, at which point the crowd, or sometimes the matador, may call for a pardon to the president, just before the kill. Goring the matador would not be considered noble!

** Portuguese bullfighting legally forbids the killing of the bull in the bullring by the matador. Instead a fake kill is made. However, the bull is led to his death straight after the corrida to the back of the plaza to be slaughtered in private.

Mario & Lazaro

Capes & Swords

Lazaro and Mario are students of the Bullfighting School in Malaga City. In their late teens, they have some experience in the ring and were keen to show me how to use the capes and swords and what they mean in a bullfight.

Explain how to use the capes.

Yes, the capote, the *muleta*... Well, the capote (the large magenta and yellow cape) was invented for those situations when the bulls came out with great force so you can slow them a bit and stop them being so violent. Bulls are slowed in this way as you never know how the bull is coming out, in what direction; using the capote you can guide the path the bull will follow, you can "drive" it. Whenever you see the bull is ready to start, the bullfighter stands like this (shows the position with his feet), and then to make the bull know where to go you extend this hand (he extends his right hand) so the bull follows it and it's then that you are actually bullfighting! Same to the other side; you take out your left hand to show the bull where to run. As you guys say, shall we continue with the "capote" or –

La muleta!

Formerly, many years ago, the muleta was used to prepare the bulls whenever they were ready to be killed, but over the years its usage has been refined to make it more elegant and beautiful, to make the passes with the bull, to kill them. Because if the bull is not aligned, it won't charge, so you must always have the bull in front, so it can't see the muleta, then you aim for the bull's horn, and when you call, the bull comes charging.

The round usually finishes with a chest pass; you usually take it on the right side, and whenever you do it you turn around and take the bull to hit him on the top. Well, you also have the left hand, that's the same as the right hand, but in this way it's more dangerous for the bullfighter, as then with the right hand you can make the sword and the muleta go wider, but not with the left hand as we can see (demonstrates a more shallow pass). Whenever a bullfighter uses the left side, it is in a certain way more important; whenever you bullfight with the left hand is more important than with the right hand. To do the finishing pass with the left hand is exactly the same as with the right hand; you finish the muleta pass, you leave it there, turn around and you hit the bull from the top. Whenever you a preparing the bull for the kill you usually do two or three muleta passes, then the bull starts surrendering; you usually do it twice or three times low down to make the bull lower the head to prepare it to be killed. Once you see the bull is ready, you usually place yourself at this distance (he stands in the ring showing the distance) more or less; we normally stand facing our side to the bull; we stand like this (stands in the bullring) then we do this (shuffles his feet) Once you enter to kill you always have the muleta in front of the bull and at the same time as the muleta, the front foot and the sword going forward. Once you move the foot in front you put the muleta on top of the bull's face so the bull only sees the muleta; that is when you go with the sword, supposedly, puf! You plunge the sword into the bull!

The moment of truth, (the moment of the kill) what are your thoughts?

Whenever I'm going to kill it – I have killed three little bulls, three little bulls already – I always, whenever I'm about to kill, whenever I'm in that moment, I just think to kill it.

Nothing else?

Nothing else!

Eyes and head closed...only...

Yes, just to kill, because if I ever think I'll be caught, or I can get hurt, a bull 'trick' or something, then I become more worried, anything, you know? I think all bullfighters, whenever we are ready to kill the bull, whatever happens, we have to kill it. Well, even more for someone who did a very good *faena*, after cutting both ears, if you prick (not get the sword in properly)...goodbye, so...

Faena muy buena (A good job with the last passes), a possibility of two ears, but a mistake with the sword and the trophy of ears is taken away.

Yes, that's it, that's why it's called the *supreme round*, because there you get the ears but also they can be taken away. *(If you miss with the sword)*

Do you train much?

Yes but not here, in my house, in the *campo*, I have something similar to that (pointing to the *carretón* outside the camera view) and yes, I train a lot.

How many days with the toreo? Seven days a week? Every day?

No, no, I train <u>ten</u> days a week! You have to train ten days a week, not seven, ten! The days I have to go to the school I come here with Fernando... (Cámara Castro, the *maestro*, or teacher) but then in the *campo* I train Tuesday, Thursday, Saturday and Sunday. Well every now and then I have to spend a Sunday with my *parienta*! (meaning girlfriend)

Same for you, Mario? You aren't worried about the kill...?

You may be worried the day before, thinking about a good faena and then a prick and that's it, but you should always think that everything's going to be alright. You should always think everything's going to be alright.

Bob Rule

Bob Rule was one of the first true aficionados I met on my quest to discover more about bullfighting. He works in the *cuadrilla*, the squad, of English matador Frank Evans as the sword carrier, known as the *Mozo De Espadas*. He lives in Granada. He became the producer for my documentary when he became the source of all contacts and knowledge for my interviews. He has been involved in bullfighting for more than thirty years and belongs to Club Taurino London.

"I have always said, though a little tongue in cheek, that the *Mozo de Espadas* is the guy who works the longest and hardest but is the only one not to stand in front of the bull, unless it gets in the *callejon* of course. So I thought a little list of jobs may be of use to those thinking about taking up the profession.

It can begin by finding out the taurine hotels at your destination and booking the appropriate number of rooms, as *cuadrillas* are not welcome in all hotels as they leave behind such a mess: blood, sand etc., and towels have gone missing! It has been said that some rooms have virtually been gutted, but like always, that is very much the minority, but they are a bit of a mess as you can imagine after a hot, sweaty and bloody *corrida*. Some hotels of course welcome the toreros as it does bring extra clients to the bar. When calculating the number of beds needed, the Mozo is not included at my level; I am not sure about the top boys. It is necessary to be at the ring for twelve o'clock for the *sorteo*, but more to see the *Guardia Civil* and hand over the *boletínes* which each member of the team must fill in with their name and social security number and show your *carnet professional* plus wages. It is the Guardia that takes over the show at this point.

Leaving after a corrida is sometimes a rush and if you are performing the following day you must check the capes and *muleta*, and brush and clean them before leaving your home, hotel or wherever you may be. Even if not fighting the next day they will need cleaning at some point. At these functions, the *impresario*, if a nice chap, will be looking for you to give you the wages for the *peones* and yourself, whom you will pay (or it may be you will have to look for him!)

You may be at the ring for an hour before going to the hotel, it will now depend on who wants to use the beds and rest, if you are lucky you may be able to nick a bed for a short while, or maybe not. This is now a long, boring time you have to kill; up to four or five hours. I have walked around villages in searing heat; it is advisable to stay out of the bars apart from maybe a snack. I have found a shady bit of grass on a factory estate and tried to sleep, I have slept in hotel receptions or wherever you can get some rest. You will of course have laid out the *traje* for the day in the bedroom before departing, making sure you have all items needed, buttons are not torn off etc.

At an agreed time, you will return to the room for the dressing, having bought sufficient water for the day both for drinking and cleaning the swords. The dressing is a fairly tranquil time; maybe an odd nervous quip and off to the ring.

At the ring, you hope it is your lucky day and have an *Ayuda Mozo de Espadas*, but more often than not at our level, no. So you get everything you can carry: two zip-up bags with capes and muletas if your torero wants everything in the ring (you hope not, so you can get two capes and three *muletas* in one bag), you also hope one will do for two swords, two *ayudas,* one *descabello*, as you also have a bit of first aid kit and the water and towels, possibly from the hotel room (I did not say that!)

While the matadors and *peones* take the accolades as they enter the ring, the mozo will be lugging all the equipment round the *callejon* to his station. After putting out your equipment you start by meeting your torero underneath the president's box after the parade, giving him his cape. While he is using the cape with his first bull you follow him round the callejon with a spare cape and some water and of course his muleta and ayuda. Dumping his cape, you quickly get a spare muleta, spare ayuda, the killing sword and descabello and follow him wherever he goes. Oh, and don't forget the water and the broom of course! After your man has done, you must clean the sword quickly before the blood dries. If it is his last bull you can begin packing up but not completely because if he is Senior Sword (whoever took his *alternativa* first), which is quite often in my case with Frank Evans, he may be called upon to kill someone else's bull should they have been gored.

Back at the hotel, the hot, sweaty and blood stained clothes all come off and the room soon looks like a tip as you pack all the clothes away to go to the cleaners, or some to be washed at home, while your man takes a shower. Then make a start getting them to the car; may be two or three trips, and to be sure there will be something in the car your man wants. A hot dusty day and you are dying for a beer but you will be the last one to finish work and the others in the team will already be having their cool drink. But you may have to drive, so the beer may have to wait. During the course of day, if there are any small jobs to be done, i.e. go and see if so-and-so is at the bar, or can you go and get that for me, or make sure X people get the tickets your man has promised; also obtain the tickets in the first place from the impresario as the case may be. The peons will also expect you to look after their things; nearly impossible if you are working solo. You may well get badgered by the public to organise photos for them and many more little things on the side: going to the garage for petrol, getting bits for the first aid kit, where does it stop?

As I said at the start, the Mozo works the hardest on fight day, so maybe not so tongue in cheek after all; although it is not good, the Mozo can get away with a slip-up, whereas with the Matador a slip-up could be costly or fatal. If you are with a top torero with a bottomless pit of money and there are two of you I am sure it is much easier, but not half as interesting! I do enjoy it really!"

Miguel Perea

Picadores

Bob and I went to Torremolinos bullring to wait for Miguel. Many cars drove up to park, but none were Miguel. Bob wasn't sure it was the bloke he knew, and I had only seen a photo of him in his picador costume. Then suddenly, a car charged straight for us, as if it wouldn't stop! I said, "I bet that's him." There is something wonderfully direct about a picador, and Miguel is no exception. He gave one of the best monologues to camera I ever had on film! (Oye, Miguel, you should be on TV, hombre!) Despite not speaking a word of English, and my Spanish then appalling, somehow we managed to have a great afternoon chatting in the bullring and then after in Los Pinos, a gladed area away from the gaudy town centre, in an old fashioned tapas bar where I was encouraged to eat a whole serving plate of strong Manchego cheese, the nearest thing to vegetarian they could find! Anyone who has eaten just the usual *tapita* of Manchego will tell you this is a mean feat indeed!

Tell me about yourself.

My name is Miguel Perea, picador of bulls since 1994, going under the orders of many matadors of bullfighting such as Jose Luis Galloso, Luis Miguel, Espartaco, including many good ones, Fernando Cámara, the maestro Frank Evans.

So, the subject today is to explain the how when and why of picadors. Picadors started at the beginning of the century and went from there. They gave the toreros their orders then; that changed a lot over time and this now is the contrary; now the picadors are under the orders of the matadors.

The thing is that the bulls come out with much violence, come out very strong and usually to 'pic' the bull makes it more calm, to make it bleed a bit, so that the bull makes a connection with the matador and there is nobility and honour in both directions. The bull is *pic'ed* a little, to take it by force, so there becomes congeniality between the toreros and the bull, and the bull has a calmer charge, so the blood is not congested, and that's when you get to the task of art and feeling, which is what everyone wants to see here in Spain.

So, to explain, that in the past, the bull was pic'ed to reduce its violence, now instead it is to attune the bull. Times have changed a lot, matadors have changed, corridas have changed, and everything has changed according to history, according to the ages, and that's all I can say about the history of the picadores.

Now another matter of the picadors, I will explain. Where I did the pic'ing, for example. When I became a picador in '94, I wanted to become a *rejoneador*, but as there was no chance of this without a horse, one day I was invited to join a *tentadero* and this resulted in me enjoying the pic'ing of a cow, a heifer, and there I was picking up friendships with matadors, and *novilleros*. Then I debuted as a picador in Las Lagunas de Mijas, in a bullring here in Malaga, and then I came with many more bullfighters as I said before; my story is from 1994 and God willing, it will continue for a long time.

The Bull and The Ban

Tell us your view on Catalonia.

What I want to say is that for sure the politicians, and whoever was involved in the bullfighting ban, have never watched a bullfight, they don't know what it's about. That's my opinion. If they saw it, then they wouldn't cause that kind of damage to the *fiesta nacional*, that's what I think. I think people involved in that, they have never seen a bullfight, they have never being to a *finca*, they don't know what a toro bravo is or the time it takes breeding them, moving to the corrals, they have no idea about what the *fiesta nacional* is, and it's because of that they ban it, because they have never seen it in their whole life.

I will give you my comments on Barcelona, what I think has happened in Catalonia. What has happened is more political than about bullfighting, it was a matter of policy and is a matter that will do enough damage in Spain because there are several provinces – several provinces who already want to remove the bullring. Being a political issue, it has damaged a lot, not just for the owners but for those who live there: the drivers, the breeders, herdsmen, cowboys, stables, grounds men, *murilleros*, and many other people, that thanks to the bulls, make their living with the bulls; the truth is then, it was a bad move for the world of the bull.

We hope, now there is a political change in Catalonia, bullfighting will return to all Catalonia, at least to Barcelona, which is a Grade One ring, with a high category, very old, where there has been many bullfights for many, many years. I tell you, there were three fights a week, on Thursdays, Saturday and Sunday, and the truth is, it is a real pity. Whether it is fixed or not fixed, we ask that bullfighting people don't spend any more (money or time) in that community (Catalonia).

Anti-taurinos say the horse suffers a lot in the ring. What do you think?

The horse of the picador nowadays doesn't suffer at all; it's been a very long time since a horse died due to the suerte de varas, as the horse is now very well protected. There are many anti-taurinos also that complain about the *puyazos*, that hurt the bull; the bull doesn't – if we compare the *puya* of 10 centimetres, now reduced to 8; to a bull that weighs 580 to 600 kilograms, it's similar to a pinprick for a human; we are talking about how the anti-taurinos have no idea of what they are talking about, and don't know what they are saying, the puyazo is a minimal damage for the bull, and we can see, in the puyazo we can see if the bull is brave or not. If the bull is brave then it comes back to the horse, if not, it doesn't, but then you don't 'pic' the bull anymore. Then how the *suerte de varas* goes, depends on how the bull wants it; if the bull is brave, then we pic it, and if not, we just stop pic'ing it, and that's my opinion, that the bull doesn't suffer as much as people say; you can see there are some bulls pardoned after 4 or 5 puyazos, or even 7, then they live, they don't die, they are healed and then they live. That is my opinion about the suerte de varas and the puyazo.

I'll briefly explain about the horses of the picador. The horses of the picador, as we the picadores travel so much, are not taken with us; the horses of the picador are used between each company in each city, as each city has one; Bilbao has one, there are three in France, in Spain each city has one, Malaga has one, Sevilla has one, Granada has one, there's another one in Jerez, so that each city has their own stables as we couldn't travel with them. The process any *caballo de picar* has to follow will be to start in the finca with cows, then after that they train with heifers and then steers, and then in the fields, after that the horses, the selected ones, go to the stables to be finally prepared for the bullrings. That's the training the horses have.

The training the picadores have is pretty similar, they start in the finca; also we have to prepare ourselves a bit, like, walking, not smoking, drink alcoholic drinks as little as possible; then in the finca we first go with the calves, then with the males, after that closed bullfights in the farms, and we do all this during the winter to be prepared for the coming season.

Banderillas

El Fandi - Granada

Emilio

Emilio is a banderillero from Malaga. We meet at La Malagueta, Malaga's Plaza de Toros during a training session with a *taurina*, a bull's head on a cart with soft padding on top to practice placing the *banderillas*, an art form in itself as a banderillero must have the nerve to run up to the bull and stick the banderilla into the animal's *murillo*. Some matadors, such as El Fandi and Paquirri place these themselves but often a cuadrilla will have banderilleros to place the sticks for the matador.

So start with the banderillas, the corrida with banderillas...

Well, the banderillero's job in the world of bulls; it's a beautiful *tercio*, but there are a few who like it and some others who don't, because the bull is pricked. But it's always good because the bull, as you may well know, whenever the bull finishes the horse (picador) round, well, it ends 'congested' (slowed down), and the banderillas then reanimate the bull, so it's fundamental, the banderillas third is fundamental. The job in fact is lovely for me, I like it because in fact I chose it many years ago, even when I had another job, because I like it, I like the risk, seems that the banderillas third doesn't, but it does has a little more risk, doesn't it? You face combat with the bull. And well, just that, it's fundamental.

A bit about the bull...

Yeah, well, let's say, while you are dealing with the bull, there were those who argued something about what else the *peones* could do, and how? Then the idea of the banderilleros grew. I think it is a bit like that. Of course, yeah, it also influences the *novilladas* without horses, as the banderillas make the bull surrender a bit, of course, it becomes weaker too. With a pricked bull it reanimates it, and with a young bull without a horse phase, which is the non-pic'ed bull, it surrenders a bit because it starts bleeding, then it goes more decongested to the muleta; that is what I think it does.

Catalonia?

I think the same as what always has been said, the bullfighting professionals talk about the people against the world of the bull, and I respect their way to think, but they have to think it as well and respect us. If we respect them, they must respect us. There are those who gave more arguments in Catalonia, have protested more so the bullfighting is banned there, I think they are wrong because it's not what the bullfighter does with the animal, as they say the animal suffers, but it's simply an art that is historical, for many years in Spain and Latin America, and beyond that you have to think it provides a lot of work; it provides a lot of jobs, many families have something to eat because of the bull's business, and that's what they haven't thought about. It has been said that the bull business will exist up to 2012 only. In my opinion, and this is what I think, they will continue even after that, I think in that way.

Fernando Cámara Castro

Fernando, a former matador, was kind enough to let me film at the Bullfighting School, which he runs. He was such a quiet person that I was blown away with his eloquent prose when asked about "La Expresion", or the face that bullfighters often make during a bullfight. I understood at that moment how intensely passionate the feeling for "los toros" can be.

Within bullfighting and flamenco, feelings are shown; the bullfighter has to express to *el publico* and also feel all at once what he does; when he feels he expresses it in the face, makes gestures of challenge; challenge and anger, so he doesn't lose the spirit of the fight. The fight and that expression the bullfighter has, that's why they stand fast, making gestures of anger and expression. They feel, they internalise, they internalise what they feel. Depending on the expression the bullfighter has, there are bullfighters that are much more expressive than others. A bullfighter with good expressions is a natural; a bullfighter fighting like this, (moves the capote with a blank face) is blank.

You must internalise what you feel. It is a set of everything: fear, courage, superiority, a full range of everything. All that must be internalised. It's not new; that's why bullfighting is a primitive expression, it's a primitive expression. It's an expression about the fight for predation, food; a fight against a wild animal. The human prevails over the wild animal, but being a man, is physically weaker than the animal; he must make use of his intelligence, and the bullfighter expresses that in the ring. It's theatre, the bullfighter must capture the whole essence of bullfighting history. That is the expression. It's the representation. It's creating an artistic expression, yet with a connotation of the fight. It's a natural expression that appears, that you get, that you acquire while you practice, while you internalise all that you feel.

Francisco Rivera Ordóñez

Francisco Rivera Ordóñez is a world famous matador often in the *Prensa Rosa*, along with his brother, also a matador, Cayetano. His family is purebred bullfighting stock: his father, Francisco Rivera (Paquirri), was a bullfighter and national treasure before being fatally gored by a bull in 1984. His grandfather, Antonio Ordóñez, was also something of a celebrity bullfighter and a great friend of Orson Welles, whose ashes are interred in an old well upon the Ordóñez country estate in Ronda, Andalusia. Fran was the subject of a book: "Death and the Sun: A Matador's Season in the Heart of Spain," by American journalist, Edward Lewine. I read this book in London before I moved to Spain, and it was my first glimpse into the world of the matador.

Fran appears at the door about an hour late, in casual pants and t-shirt, munching a croissant. But his lateness is understandable: he just travelled fifteen hours overnight in a van from a bullfight up north to Malaga for the *feria*, and he slept around three hours. In person, he seems smaller than I perceive him in the bullring with his bulky *traje de luces*, but younger; more athletic and vital, and definitely more handsome. He apologises profusely and is immediately intent on making everyone feel comfortable for the interview despite how tired he must feel himself. He says he wants to try the interview in English, to practise. He doesn't have many English friends, he says, and it's a good opportunity for him. I have transcribed the interview as spoken, because it gives the reader a true appreciation for the way Fran speaks: he sees and hears what he describes, and shares feelings as they form. So I didn't try to correct pauses, or imperfections in his excellent English as some editors

would in this text, because the subjects we talk about are so deeply personal to him and his family. I want to find out what he thinks of those people that are changing the world he has always known.

In Britain and other countries, there is a perception that bullfighting is on its way out, partially due to the coverage in media about Catalonia and the ban that is coming next year. Why do you think this is?

Well, I don't know the truth really what happened, I don't know exactly. I think it's when the politics comes to somewhere, it breaks everything, you know. Because when we go to fight in Catalonia in some places, the people liked it, we only say, "OK you don't like bullfighting, OK, we respect you, you have to respect us." It's very confused, it's very... it's a big problem because make people get angry, confused, many people don't understand what happened, but I think it's a politics way to... you know, I hope we don't go to nowhere in that way, I hope everything calms down in Catalonia also, let's see, let's see what happens.

In Article 6, the paper that they created, they have a clause, as an exception, in the paper, that says that they will ban bullfights but they are making an exception for the festival bulls, the bull running, you know...

Yeah, that looks like a joke. I prefer to see a bull in the ring, I think it's more honour, you know, fighting the bull, it's a big honour for the bull, a big honour for the bullfighter, the bull really has a choice to race for his life, because if he does it very good, you can save the bull's life. Sometimes happens, not a lot, but sometimes happens. And I think it's different, because for every bullfighter, every bull we fight, is part of us. I don't like seeing those bulls running, being (makes stabbing motion)... You know, tied, burning his horns... I don't like that, I prefer seeing a bull in the ring, beautiful, an audience, and see what the bullfighter can do, I think is very, very different, so when some politics guy says, "OK we don't like the bullfight but we like this kind of thing", it looks like a joke, really.

I've been filming in the bullfighting school; I'm meeting lots of young people that get involved with the corrida. And in the same article in Catalonia, they say that children under 14 years old are now banned from going to see the bullfight. Now when I go, I see big families together, from babies to old people, and so they say that, well, the quote was "the witnessing of a violent act was seeing to have a negative emotional effect on the..."

No, that's not true, that's, that's stupid, that's not true, I go to bullfights when I was very, very young. I brought my daughter when she was small. I saw many friends bringing his kids, and that's stupid, that's a stupid thing. I think if someone loves the bull, it's bullfighters, and the people who like the bullfight, *love*, we *really* love the bull and we fight and we kill him because we love fighting and we have to kill him. We don't like it really, we don't like the dying. The bull dies and we are happy? No, it's not, it's very special, I know it's difficult to understand us maybe, but we are not happy when the bull dies, we are happy with the bull (being) brave, when the bull attacks... he attacks, and show us he is noble, how brave he is, that's what we really love, and the bullfight has many, many things from deep inside; the tragedy, all the kids coming, grandfathers, fathers, kids, you know, it's a big history and respect. There are many points in the ring (that) is good for a child I think. And that's stupid, I don't like that law.

And what do you think would happen to Andalusia if the bullfighting ban was brought here?

Well I don't know, I don't want to think about that really; a very big problem not even in Andalusia but around Spain because there's a lot, *a lot* of people working in the bullfight; the bullfighter, many people around us. I don't know how many people in Spain, thousands or a *million*, working in bullfights. So if that happens, Spain is going to have a big, big problem really and the bull...if the bullfighter doesn't exist, there's no way to exist; it's stupid to have a bull because bull is a creation, you know, you have to keep that. You have to take a fight with one bull, fight a cow, if they both are good they can have a small bull, a small bull that you have to take care of for four years in a ranch, take care of him with the veterinaries, with food, with *everything* and the cow you have to fight, make an exam, see if the cow is good, then you leave it for breeding; so it's hard work. If the bullfighter doesn't exist, the bull is no way going to exist, we are going to take the bull. "OK we don't like that, take it out?" That's, I don't know, that's crazy.

I have both anti-taurinos as well as bullfighters in my film, and one point many bring up is that bullfighting only carries on because of tourism, but my experience, every corrida that I go to, sometimes I'm one of very few foreigners in the ring, so why do you think that the perception outside Spain is that it's only for tourism?

That's not true, that's not true, maybe in a couple of rings, close to the sea, maybe you can find a lot of foreigners, but the people who go to the fights are people from Spain, that's the truth, that's reality. Of course if you are looking for someone who knows about the world, "Spain, Oh Spain, flamenco and bullfight!" That's it, that is true too, so why not? Bullfighting is from us, really from deep inside, the bullfighting started in Spain and we bring it to South America and France, Southern French, but the bulls, bullfight is, you know, something very Spanish, and around the world, they know about Spain and the bullfight. I like it; I think it is good.

Why do you think this tradition is so important to Spain?

Bullfighting is a big tradition, it has many, many years, changed a little, not a lot, because really I think that the bullfight − maybe you hate it, maybe you go and you go "Oh my god, this is horrible", or maybe you go and like it, but it's bullfighting − is something different than everything, there's nothing like the bullfight. Seriously, you can feel emotions, you can feel the colours, the people, it's a very, very, *very* special game of death maybe, you only can find here. This is us, this is real, the bull dies but sometimes the bullfighter dies too, and it's something, you know, it's very difficult to explain, it's something that you have to go see; maybe you don't like it, but maybe you can find something and you're going to say "Oh, my god, these guys are crazy!" Maybe, or whatever, this is special and this is different, the bullfight is different than everything, that's the truth.

I think one thing that is very difficult for a foreign person to understand and maybe some people that watch the film would not understand is how you as a person feel when you make the kill and what I would like to know is how you feel after you make the kill and the bull is dying, what are you thinking about? I've seen you in the ring and you are very nice with the bull at that point, very calm and spiritual – so what are you thinking?

It's difficult to explain. It's difficult to explain to someone that I killed a bull but I don't really want to kill him, or I'm not happy to kill him, I have to kill him and I try to kill him correctly and fast, you know. I don't want the bull to have a bad time, I don't want to be cruel for the bull, because I love the bull really, and it's very... I know, it's impossible to understand; you say "OK you love the bull and you kill him, I don't understand that". It's difficult to explain, but it's like that, you know, so we kill him because we have to kill him. I fought already more than, I don't know, one thousand, almost three hundred fights maybe, so I kill, fight and kill more than two thousand, I don't know, five hundred bulls. But what I like is the fight really, and I can remember each bull I fought, every one, it's a part of me, and everything I have is coming from the bull, so I really love the bull, I have to kill them, and sometimes if the bull is very good, I feel sad, I don't want to kill him. I have to, because I do it, but I don't really like it, and I feel sometimes sad. I know is very difficult to explain and difficult to understand, you know, but we are not always happy to kill the bull we have in front of us. The bull has to be our friend, when the bull is our enemy we are in trouble! The bull has got to be our friend but the bull has to want it, and has to attack us and try to kill us; if the bull doesn't like the ring fight we are in trouble. We need that bull that really wants to attack, really. We really need that he really wants to kill us, that is good for us, and that makes it emotional, that makes, you know... But that bull is our friend, it's very difficult.

So I was just going to say, so when you have a bull that doesn't want to attack you, it's... sad for you...

Very sad, that breaks our nerves, it's very difficult for us, we don't like that.

And, therefore in rings where they don't kill the bull, like in Portugal, do you think there's any value to the corrida when you don't kill at the end? Do you think this is less cruel or has any value?

I don't know, I don't know, you don't kill the bull inside the ring but you kill it when the bull goes back. I don't understand the bullfight with no kill for the bull. My great grandfather was a bullfighter and my grandfather, and my uncles, my father, cousins, brother; I don't understand the fight like that. Maybe we can see, we can study, we can...but I think it's more noble for the bull killed in the ring: I attack him, he attacks me, it's...you know, better than not getting him and then Pum! (Makes an action like the air pistol) I don't like that for the bulls too, I think it's not a noble death. My father died in the ring; it was an accident, you know, because he's a bullfighter, so I'm sure if... let's say, God is coming and says, "You have to die tomorrow, how do you want to die, in a car accident or in a ring?" I'm sure that my father would say, "In a ring, of course." I think if you ask a bull, he's going to say the same. "I prefer to die in a ring", I'm sure of that.

How do you see the future for bullfighting?

I see it with a good smile, really, because you can fight seventy days a year, so I see many rings, many people and you can see a lot of kids, young people in the ring. I think it's a good time for fights, very good fighters, a lot, you can find very, very good fighters; the bull is incredible right now, I think it is a very good time for bullfights. And I *hope*, and I hope, everything becomes calm and, like we respect the people who don't like it, we want that they respect us. You don't like the bullfight? OK, don't go, don't worry! I don't like soccer, I don't go!

The Bull and The Ban

Frank "El Ingles" Evans

Frank Evans is probably the most well-known bullfighter to a UK reader. He was the subject of a Channel 4 documentary, "Bus Pass Bullfighter" and has written a book about his experiences, "The Last British Bullfighter". The son of a Salford butcher, Frank decided to become a matador when he read about another British matador, Vincent Charles Hitchcock. As a young man, he would practise in the local park until finally he went to Spain and stunned audiences with his skills, gaining matador status in 1991. He plans a comeback after recovering from heart bypass surgery and a new knee this year. We meet in a bar in Fuengirola, which is decked with photos of Frank's bullfights. Talking with Frank Evans you feel you are talking to a real star: the room lights up when he enters and he has a presence which I imagine can be very useful in a corrida. He has also had a lot of attacks from animal activists on his home and family, which is another side to the debate I am interested in learning about.

Do you think that a ban will ever happen in Andalusia, like it's happened in Catalonia?

Well, I don't think so, because Catalonia is a completely different 'kettle of fish' if you like, to Andalusia. I think that when we think about the ban that's taken place in Catalonia, you have to look a little bit deeper and a bit further behind the actual ban itself because Catalonia regards itself as a separate nation to Spain.

They've done away with the Spanish flag, they have their own flag. They've done away with the Spanish language, they have their own language. So they were going to get rid of the bullfight, because it sort of represents, in their opinion, something which is Spanish and it refers really to General Franco's forty years. He was a dictator here and he treated them very badly; I mean, shortly after the Civil War he killed millions of Catalans because they were against his attempt to become the dictator of Spain. You can understand the resentment that continues there from the Civil War, and I think that the people who are against bullfighting have had a ride on the back of nationalism. Bullfighting isn't really a natural thing in that part of the world, so had they tried to get it banned purely and simply on animal rights terms, I don't think they would have succeeded.

One of the problems I have with outright bans is that if you look at bullfighting in its entirety, you won't be able to say it's all bad. I would say, for example, the way we rear the animals is almost perfect. The bulls live until full maturity: four, five years. They're bred on open plains and the sierras. They're looked after by dedicated cowboys, veterinary surgeons, their nutrition is perfect. These are thoroughbred animals, which are reared in captivity as well as you could do it. The way they're transported to the bullring is meticulous and scrupulous. Until they come into the bullring, I don't think you can put any question mark over the way people in bullfighting conduct themselves. It employs hundreds of thousands of people. It helps the economy. It provides a cultural background for some people here in this country.

When it comes to what happens in the bullring, I personally feel that I can defend all of it, apart from the kill. There are moves here in Spain, I took part recently in

123

a debate, taurine people, where there are moves to alter the law governing the kill of the bull. The law at the moment requires the matador to kill the bull with a sword from the front, and it's one of the most difficult things in life to do and 99% of human beings are not capable of doing it, and unfortunately, because of incompetence, and because it's such a difficult skill to acquire, I'm not saying rarely, but very often, the bull doesn't die under one sword thrust quickly. I think you could almost say, well, let the matador attempt twice or maybe three times, because the other point is that if your work has been exemplary and you kill with one sword thrust, you will gain the trophy. If you miss with the sword, you lose the trophy. So to continue with the sword really has no point, and all that happens then is that the animal is suffering.

I've seen occasions when incompetent matadors have tried to kill a bull three, four, five, ten times; and they're massacring the bull then. I think we should alter that; give the matador one attempt or two attempts with the sword, and if he's not killed it with one sword thrust, then bring out the air pistol, like you do in the slaughterhouse, and shoot the bull.

How does it make you feel when you actually go for the kill – the moment of truth?

From a matador's point of view, the kill puts such pressure upon you. If you stand in front of a fighting bull, you have to approach the bull from the front. It's not terrorising, but it puts you under tremendous stress; it tests.

If there were no horns on the bull, I'm sure we would all want to put the sword in first time, but because there is this great danger, there's a little man inside of you trying to pull you out of the way, and if you go offline, the sword doesn't go in. The only way the sword goes in is if you go in behind the sword, and you need great decision and great technique to do that.

I would say of course that the people who criticise the killing of the fighting bull, I've never heard them criticise what takes place in what they think are civilised communities.

In the UK for example, we kill just under one million animals a day for the food chain, and fifty percent of those animals are killed by the halal method, which means that the animal is taken into the slaughterhouse and it has its throat cut, and it's simply left to die. I'm not necessarily criticising that, but I'm criticising the hypocrisy of people who point the finger at bullfighting but never say anything about that which is taking place – and I'm English, so I'm talking about the English people – it takes place in the UK. Apart from the way the animals are killed in the UK, a cow or a bull for example will live six, seven, eight months in a factory, it won't see the light of day, and the life of the animals which are bred for the food chain is inferior to the life of the fighting bull.

Some of the arguments would be that, as in fox hunting, when they do drag hunting, they don't actually kill the fox they just have the entertainment of the sport. Can you ever see that being applied in bullfighting, and if so, what do you think would happen to the breeds that are bred for bullfighting if they weren't going to be killed in the ring?

Well, the breeding of fighting bulls is a very expensive business. I don't think many breeders actually make much money from doing it. It's almost like breeding racehorses; you've got to go into it and expect not to make money, but they do it because they have great love of the activity, probably very wealthy. If bullfighting didn't take place, the breeders of bulls would definitely disappear, because nobody would be able to sustain the enormous costs of breeding fighting cattle just for the sake of breeding them. With regard to not killing the bull, they've already done that for example in Portugal and bullfighting isn't watched by anybody. You see, all that you do in the bullring with the cape, with the picador, with the muleta, is so that you can put the sword in. It's all a build up to the kill.

We call it, in English, a 'bull fight', which gives people the wrong impression immediately. The Spanish call it a 'running of the bulls'. The bull is run on the end of a cloth until he is tired and stands still in a position to have a sword delivered. So, if you don't kill him at the end, there is no point in doing all the other things. It's pointless. I could say, what is the point in foreplay before you make love to a young lady if you're not going to do it at the end?

There's really no point to it at all and there is a frustration there at the end of that if you do that, so I don't believe you'll ever see bullfighting in Spain without the kill at the end of the bullfight.

The Bull and The Ban

Do you think there's been a decline in interest from young people? What's been your experience with young people and bullfighting?

In my experience, I've never really noticed what I would describe as young people in the audience at bullfights. I've been watching bullfights since the early sixties and there has always been maybe a twenty-five percent element of younger people. It seems to be the mature people who are watching the bullfight. You've also got to differentiate; if you go and watch a bullfight in Madrid or Seville, in the major bullrings in the major ferias, it's quite expensive; it's quite strict and serious, if you like.

The older people seem to go with the suits on, with the very well dressed wife or girlfriend. It's an occasion. But if you now go into a village, go down to the small towns in Spain where there's much more bullfighting taking place than there are in the major cities, then it's fiesta time then and people will come with a completely different dress, much more casually dressed. They usually bring beer, food, cheese, wine, and the kids go and there's more than one band, impromptu bands, and they come to have a good time, and you will see the whole of the facade of the age groups; you see children, teenagers, older people, because it's more of a community activity when you go off the major cities.

So do you think that this community side to bullfighting, if we lost that, it would really affect Spain's culture, like in England, we've lost our things that we did like Morris dancing and the maypoles – all these kinds of things that

127

we probably did when we were children are now gone, because of the Internet and clubbing and all these kinds of things. Do you see that happening in Spain?

It's difficult for me to envisage what will happen in the future in Spain.

Change in Spain does seem to take a long time and it's very slow to alter and become 'Europeanised' if you like. I'm sure it's better for Spain that it doesn't try and imitate other countries in its way of behaving. One of the things about the bullfighting debate is that you seem to have people who are passionately in favour of it who support it and take part in it, and the other lot who are totally against it, and I would describe them as abolitionists. We need somebody in the middle here to say look let's just alter some things, so that you'll be happy with it carrying on, and the people who are against it won't mind in carrying on. We don't have to ban things altogether, because as I said earlier on, bullfighting isn't all bad. I'll hold my hands up and say there are one or two things. I would be happier if minor changes were made, they would have a major effect I think. But I'm quite sure that if we didn't kill the bull the way we do, I could defend bullfighting to the death. I would have no problem justifying all that we do. But I can't justify the kill if it's not quick.

I would like to see the bullfighting people, the authorities, we who handle and manipulate and control and run bullfighting, make the changes. If you look back over the last one hundred and fifty years, I know that around about eighteen-fifty something, the first animal rights activist group against bullfighting was formed somewhere in Almeria I think it was, and they've gone this one hundred and fifty plus years without affecting one single change. I know what's happened in Catalonia, but that was always going to happen there anyway. But they've made no material changes to what happens in the bullfight. So, they've got it wrong too, because if the bull needs help, god help the bull that he's got them working for them because they're ineffective people. But there have been changes, for example, in 1928, it was decided by the veterinary scientists that the bull was fully mature at four, so his age was altered. 1930 was the first time they put the padding on the horse, so the horses stopped getting killed. 1952 they put a cross on the picador's lance; stopped him from killing the bull unnecessarily. The weight of the horse was also altered, something like ten years ago. Several changes have been made. All by us. And I think it's time for us now to look again, because if it's imposed upon us then they have the ability to do more impositions. If we do it and clean things up and make it acceptable then it will make it very hard for the animal rights people to attack us.

If you had a message for the activists: if you could speak directly to them now, what would your message be?

Over the years, I've had plenty to do with animal rights activists. Naively from my point of view, in the beginning, I thought I could sit down and reason with these people. But my own experience is that they are totally and utterly unreasonable. Ninety-nine percent of them know almost nothing about what bullfighting really is and they are extremists and they are sinister. Apart from the hate mail and other sort of harassments (sic), I've had a letter bomb sent to me and my family have been harassed and my animals. And I personally have no time whatsoever for these people, so this is why I would say I don't really need to have any debates with them, I want to work on my own people in bullfighting, get us to make the changes that I feel need to be made, and I do know what needs to be made and I know the changes that should take place in bullfighting. They don't. And make the bullfight healthy and acceptable so that they can't do harm to the bullfight, to me, or to my people.

"Indultado" bulls graze with the herd at the finca of Julio De La Puerta, in ten kilometres of woodland and plain.

The Bull

Alexander Fiske-Harrison

When I interviewed Jason Webster he told me about Alexander's book. It sounded intriguing: a young British writer travels to Spain to learn how to become a bullfighter. Alexander is also an accomplished playwright and actor, having trained at the Stella Adler Studio in New York.

We eventually meet in Seville during San Miguel, the September feria which is a date in the taurine calendar. After filming a sequence for the film, we settle in a bar, Meson Serranito, which turns out to be serendipitous. Not only is the owner happy for us to film, but he is a brilliant singer and hands me a CD of amazing taurine themed music for use in my soundtrack. The soundtrack has backing vocals by Padilla, who is Alexander's friend and the main matador discussed in his book. Alexander learned to fight and kill a bull over a period of two years, an experience documented in his book, Into The Arena.

So why do foreigners have a right to an opinion on bullfighting? We are not Spanish. Often it's argued by the Spanish that it's nobody else's business what they like to do...

The question about foreigners having a view on bullfighting is, well I mean, not least because Spain is part of the European Union, one has to. But also, if you take my case, which is someone who was very unsure what they felt about bullfighting but wasn't turned off massively by the blood and the death, which obviously some people react to very strongly; I came here to get to know it so I could explain it to an English speaking, Anglo-

Saxon as they call them, audience. There are people in Spain who think that foreigners shouldn't have an opinion on bullfighting because they find it's an imposition, it's an invasion of their morals, our cultural prejudices onto their, as they call it, *Fiesta Nacional* of bullfighting. The trouble is that Spain is part of the European Union; there are EU subsidies going into the ranches of the bulls, because they are farms, but also the bullrings are historic buildings, so they take EU subsidies to restore them and keep them in good condition. So as such, they have to deal with the outside world on this. If they don't, then it's going to get closed from outside, which is a risk, although the EU constitution has a clause preventing that, especially now as France has made it an untouchable matter of cultural heritage and soon it will made that in Spain as well.

And huge numbers of tourists attend the bullfight. It's very hard to get accurate statistics but on a good bullfight in a major town like here in Seville tonight, tomorrow night, the night after, it will be forty percent tourists, my estimate, in the ring. So there's a massive interaction with the outside world. But it is decreasing, that interaction with the outside world, because it is increasingly that the glamour of it has worn off as Western Europe and America become more animal friendly, more interested in animal welfare and to the point of taking it to animal rights as a genuine issue. Interestingly, Spain was one of the first countries to introduce rights for primates in research, which is bizarre given they have bullfighting.

So as such, you have to have an interaction with the foreigners; also the number of tourists who fill the bullrings in Spain. It's untrue to say it's entirely tourists but in Seville here tonight and tomorrow night it will probably be forty percent tourists and sixty percent Spanish. That's because there are very good bullfighters fighting. So, if you take the great ambassadors of bullfighting; the most famous is Ernest Hemingway I guess, some of the Spanish have a problem with Hemingway because they say he didn't really know about bulls or he never got into the ring himself. Most notably he made Pamplona immensely famous having never run with the bulls. But Hemingway was a great friend of many matadors and breeders, especially Juan Belmonte who was the originator of the modern bullfight.

And people have very mixed feeling about him here. He wrote his first article on bullfighting in the early twenties having never seen one, which is wonderful, but he was a man who was very capable of making things up and he did write about it very well. But if you take his later writings on bullfighting, he clearly has a deep knowledge. He began as friends with Juan Belmonte, in the, I guess, 1920s. And then Nino de la Palma, who became the matador Pedro Romero in his first novel, "The Sun Also Rises", published as, I think, "Fiesta", in England. And actually it was originally written as a short story called Cayetano Ordóñez, which was the matador's real name. And his son Antonio Ordóñez, who was best friends with Hemingway, and there's millions of photos of them together in the ring. How deep his knowledge was is arguable, but he did great things for the bullfight in terms of publicity and understanding. So the Spanish who say he was a fraud or he had no right to an opinion – they're doing themselves a disservice by saying that.

I have to say, I haven't encountered any problems; I came here to write a book about the world of the bullfight with a slightly undecided mind on whether it was right or wrong. By the end, I fought and killed a bull myself, and still I had mixed feeling about this, but I noticed the Spanish were very open to me and they were delighted – they do understand that their *fiesta nacional* is in danger, with the ban in Barcelona coming in this Sunday *(last bullfight, Sept 25, 2011)*. They understand that they have to interact with the outside world because that is one of the reasons perhaps that Barcelona instituted its ban, as it's the most international, most cosmopolitan and most progressive of the Spanish cities. And they see it as a good thing for tourism, to say 'We've banned bullfighting. You can come to us with a clear conscience". And this has mobilised a sort of counter wave of propaganda across Spain as the bullfighting industry starts to unify and become as organised as the animal welfare groups who are attacking the bullfight.

Why did you decide in your book to take on the challenge of training in the ring and then going on to kill a bull? Why did you want to do that?

When I first came up with the idea for my book, which was to answer a question about bullfighting – is it justifiable? I mean, I already had the position that given that we eat meat and we eat it not for nutritional reasons, and often it actually has a nutritionally negative value. We eat it for aesthetic reasons; we eat it for entertainment, so an animal is killed for entertainment. I didn't have an issue with bullfighting on that. But the actual infliction of pain and injury on an animal in that way – what could possibly justify this? I became more and more immersed in the world of bullfighting trying to answer that question. So I realised I had to cover the world as completely as I could. Hemingway covered it very well in "Death in the Afternoon", but very much from the audience perspective. I wanted to give all of it, so I made matador friends and they asked me to join them in the ring, so I started caping some calves, and it turned out that I could do this, I had some facility for this. And then it became 'Well now I really want to know everything about this world'.

The biggest thing of all in the world of the bullfight is the moment of truth, when the matador crosses the horns with a sword, it's when most matadors who have died in history die, and it is the only time that the bull is no longer charging the matador – the matador is charging the bull. It's a natural close to my book, but also to experience what the matador experiences – because having judged the virtue of the audience for wanting to watch it, there is also the question of the ethics of the practitioners, the ethics of the people actually fighting. Because it's one thing to say 'I'll eat meat', but it's another thing to work in an abattoir and to choose to do so, and so what exactly is the matador undergoing, what is he feeling... What I found there was – I mean this was my first kill, my only kill that I did – was the terrible pressure upon you to do it well, because you're terrified that you will screw up the job, but also that you will inflict unnecessary suffering on the animal. You are striving for a clean kill. Everything in the setup of the bullfight is designed to create a clean kill, however, because it's such a difficult technique of killing, because you go over the horns with the sword and you're entering into a letterbox between the fourth and fifth rib with the spine on one side and the clavicle of the shoulder on the other. It can be very difficult to do, and when I killed, twice I hit bone and then the sword went in. The feelings you have when that happens – it's very strange, it's a mixture, I mean, there's no jubilation, there's no joy there. There's an element of happiness in 'My God, thank God I've done this right' but also 'Thank God I'm still alive' because you're going over the horns and then passing around the side. And then there is a huge wave of sadness, and in my case, which I don't think is normal for young Spanish bullfighters training – regret. Genuine regret about what I had done. But not to the level that I would take it back.

Do you think that the people around you had enabled you to feel that that was okay, or do you think that it was genuinely okay?

In terms of, was I affected by the ethics of the people who had surrounded me for two years? Had I become influenced by their morality? No, absolutely not. I mean no question. I'm not fifteen, I'm thirty five, and I had a very clear view and maintained a very clear view of what I think is cruel in the bullfight and what I think is beautiful in the bullfight and what I think is morally permissible and what is not morally permissible. And I have not shifted on that. I eat meat; it would be ludicrous for me to sit and say that the killing of an animal for my entertainment is wrong. We're sitting in a beautiful bar here, Meson

Serranito named after Serrano ham, a pig, which is a far more intelligent, far more sociable, far more human-like animal than a bull and the man is over there carving its leg now. That animal was slaughtered, and you eat this for sheer pleasure, for entertainment, and so it would be rank hypocrisy for me to say that I have a serious issue with killing. The actuality of killing an animal that large with a sword is so personal – undeniably affects you emotionally and psychologically. But at the moral level, not the sentimental level, but the actual level of ethics, I could not claim to have a problem with that.

Can you remember what you felt at the exact moment the sword went in? Can you remember what that moment was like for you?

I think that one can be overly literary – I'm a writer – but also overly philosophical in your thoughts about what it's like to kill the bull, because at that moment in time, you are charging with a sword at a pair of horns with, in the case of my bull, 330 kilos of muscle behind it; you have no space for thought. There genuinely is nothing going on in your head other than "How do I do this?" I mean, it is an impossible task. You are placing a blade over two blades, and trying frantically to get one in whilst avoiding the other two. So when the sword went in, I was actually shocked at how easily the sword goes in having never stabbed anything before or stabbed anyone. And then, the reason why that struck me, because it meant that I was descending incredibly fast physically down towards the horn coming up towards my stomach, which meant I had to pivot round as quick as I could. But given that my feet were in the air at the time, I had very little leverage, and it was just a matter of mechanics and geometry and the instinct to survive and the instinct to kill as best you can. The emotional wash comes very much afterwards and only when you know you're clear and you're alive. I don't believe that the brain, it seems to me, does not have time to process any emotions at that time.

Would you do it again?

Would I kill a bull again? At the time, I said I wouldn't, because I didn't see the necessity. I regarded it as a piece of research vital to the book. I committed, in some senses, a sin, which was justifiable for the greater good of bullfighting. Because I believe that when a bull is killed well as part of a proper corrida de toros, it's a beautiful thing that justifies the kill. What I did was not that good, therefore it was not justified by that, it was justified by the research and the book that was the finished product. However, it has stuck in my head since, and I thought I would divorce myself from the world of the bulls afterwards, but you don't because it gets under your skin; there is nothing else like it in the world. There's nothing left existing like this in the Western world. And that peculiar combination of something that grew out of something barbaric and turned into something – it is intrinsically modern because it's an art form; I mean, it is useless, it is purposeless; it's not a sport. And as such, you get involved in the world of an art form, if your soul is sensitive to that, you are drawn in and you will not leave. And so, there are now people saying I should return to the ring, fight again, and I'm finding it increasingly difficult to say no. So I think I probably will go back into the ring but I'm not sure when.

Do you think that people who are against bullfighting, animal activists, do you think there is a certain dislocation from what death means in western society? That maybe one of the draws to bullfighting might be to witness the death of something that ultimately we will all experience, we will all die.

I think that when people take a stance against bullfighting as they do in a lot of countries in Europe and in the US, in Spain as well – there is an element of denying the reality of death. One of the functions of the bullfight is that – it is the only art form in which what it represents, it also is. It is man facing death. We all face it. He avoids it, one hopes, and in the end kills death, triumphs over it. And this is something that a lot of people don't understand because they think that bullfighting is about – well it's this terrible English word 'bullfight', that you don't have in Spanish – they think it's a man fighting an animal and its unfair because the animal always loses. The English sense of fair play. It's not. It's a tragic morality play as they used to have in the medieval era that shows you the reality of what we're all going to end up facing, and it is the only such thing in existence. Everything else is fake. Every other representation merely represents. This is why Garcia Lorca called it the last serious thing left in the world today. Because it is the last real thing. We have hidden every other representation of death. We have sterilized and sanitised. We have our hidden abattoirs. And until you have a relative who dies, you don't witness death, and normally you don't even see actual death. We are increasingly hiding ourselves from what we all face, and the bullfight brings it to you. It frames it in gold as if it were a painting, but the painting is still the dark and horrific truth – we all die. Whether the matador is death or the bull is death I don't know. By the end, they switch roles.

There's been a study of boys that go for lessons on bullfighting, and it was found that they had a higher sense of morality, and how to behave, than boys that don't. Do you think there's some kind of truth in that? Something about seeing death and witnessing it that somehow checks us into – the Spanish live life to the full much more than say British people do.

It's something that people will often say to you in Spain about bullfighting, just in England as they do about rugby – just go to a football match and see how people can behave badly. I've never witnessed any violence or crowd unrest at a bullfight. It's always conducted with utmost seriousness and dignity, and this transfers onto the bullfighters themselves, so hence, they say that the children of the bullfighting schools have greater sense of morality. Whether that's really morality or them – where does morality come from? I don't know – but there's an element of playacting dignity; they are taught that a matador must always be dignified, must always be honourable, must always conduct himself with an element of seriousness. But more than that is when you train, and not just learning the passes, but when you train with cattle, with animals from 100 kilograms up to the big bulls of Pamplona of 700 kilograms, you have a group of men around you whom you have to have absolute faith in. They will risk their life to save yours. And having that from an early age, people running in to save you, teaches you trust in tight circumstances, which will make you more moral – certainly makes the men here have a much more – one could call it a Latin expressiveness – but the affection and the esteem, which matadors hold their teams in, people in the world of the bulls hold each other in, the camaraderie is comparable to men in war or something like that. How much that justifies the bullfight, I don't know, but it does reflect back on the audience and that would to me justify the bullfight. They see something of great dignity and importance, and treat it as such. And it is open to all. It is not like going to the opera or the ballet. They're not learning their humanity from high art. Anyone can watch a bullfight and be stunned because it has all the coarse in-your-face reality of Hollywood, but contained within it all the darker and higher truths of Dostoyevsky or Shakespeare.

I find Seville very religious compared to a lot of other cities. So the fact that cities like Seville have a more religious atmosphere than others, do you think there is a connection between – for instance at Semana Santa, you often see policemen with the guys that run the rings, then you've got the Opus Dei and they're all dressed up and they're all going out together with the children. I mean, one shock for me at Semana Santa was seeing the children as Nazarenes walking around. So do you think there's any relationship between how religious the place is compared to the imagery of death that you get there and bullfighting?

Well, here in Seville you have a particularly Catholic and religious part of Spain, and also a particularly taurine, bullfighting, part of Spain; and they have become linked. I don't think that they are necessarily linked. I think the linkage is a general ambience and culture of appreciation of death. This is a hard land, and it grew out of a warlike history, and so their version of Catholicism is more interested in the Crucifixion and the Sorrow of the Virgin, than you would find in parts of Italy for example. And I think that that affects their view of bullfighting.

I do find it very strange that the way that they deal with the bull in the ring is that the bull is a protagonist in this drama and they act as though he has a soul and can be morally judged. He is a brave bull, he is a cowardly bull. He is strong or weak, noble or ignoble. And yet, they justify the bullfight by saying that the bull has no soul. So there is a contradiction there. But people are contradictory. It's intrinsically linked, but there is something, I think, pagan, about their view of bullfighting. There is an argument that it grew out of the Mithras cult of the Roman legionaries, and I increasingly agree with that theory, because it is a pagan man and death ritual, that's become a drama. And there's something slightly pagan about their form of Christianity here. The cult of the Virgin here is so much stronger than I've seen anywhere else in Latin Europe, that it speaks to me of, there's some a little more, I wouldn't say primitive, in their Christianity, but more earthy in their Christianity here and that is why it links to the bulls there, it links from the – as Garcia Lorca called it "The stones and the thistles of Andalusian soil...Only things like flamenco and bullfighting can grow as art forms out of this", and it's there; it's in the moan of the flamenco, and it's in the death of the bull, and the sacrifice of Jesus, and the sorrow of the Virgin. Blood and death and weeping. *Eso es flamenco. Eso es los toros.*

Gaspar Jiménez Fortes

Gaspar Jiménez Fortes was the impresario until recently of Benalmádena Plaza de Toros in Andalusia. He is the husband of *matadora* Mari Fortes and father of matador Jiménez Fortes. He has been involved in bullfighting all his life. He was my second interview, a chance meeting in a taurine bar in Fuengirola when he came to meet my interviewee Frank Evans, whose portrait is painted on the side of Benalmádena bullring. I spoke hardly any Spanish then, and had typed out Spanish questions on a paper in case of meeting Spanish speaking subjects along the way. He would read my question and talk at the camera, which must have been strange, knowing I understood nothing, and had no signal he had finished speaking except a gruff nod and a quick *Bueno*. He was very patient! His interview is filled with such colourful opinion; whether you agree or not with what is said, it's very interesting reading.

Do you think bullfighting has a future?

Young people have never been in a very large majority at the bullfights in Spain, but it has always been the same. It has always been the same; the penchant for bullfighting starts at twenty or twenty five years old, and well, it has always been so; a show ingrained in Spain and seven or eight more countries, and the liking for it is massive.

In Spain, for example, it is one of the primary industries creating jobs, and generates several billion euros of taxes for the country, and creates a huge revenue; there are more than ten million tickets sold yearly for bullfighting, it means more than ten million people go to bullfighting per year. I think it's really important, because young people don't go anywhere usually, neither football nor other things. They start to go once they are twenty, twenty five years old, then they start to go to bullfighting and other kinds of shows.

I think Andalusia is the same as in the rest of Spain; there are many bullfighting fans, there is a lot of stockbreeding, many thousands of hectares of land dedicated to ecological bull breeding in Andalusia, Extremadura, Salamanca; in many parts of Spain. Then we have Northern Spain, the centre, Madrid, Pais Vasco, Zaragoza, Extremadura, Valencia... there is a great interest, and in Barcelona, in Catalonia.

What do you think of the situation in Catalonia?

Specifically I think it's a political issue which has come to create this problem, because in Catalonia there is also a big bullfighting fan community, every Sunday the bullring offers a show, there are more than five or six thousand people turning up. I think that it's a political issue; our president is currently forbidding everything; smoking is forbidden in the bars, it's forbidden to go over 110 kph in the highways, he's forbidding everything! And in between he also wants to start in Catalonia, banning the bullfights. But I think there are political issues, and about Catalonia I think it's not going to happen because it's been appealed against in the constitutional court by the opposition party, the next government. And I think it's not going to happen, the bullfighting prohibition, that's what I think, among other things because the government itself has a very good source of income taxes and many thousands of people go to the bullrings. I think the issue in Catalonia won't have a major impact.

What would happen if it was banned in Andalusia?

I think that if the government tries to forbid the bullrings in Andalusia, where there are thousands and thousands of people who live from the bullfighting business, and thousands of hectares of land dedicated to bull breeding, it could happen what happened in some Arab countries: people would rise against the government. I think it's totally impossible in Andalusia, also in Extremadura and in Salamanca, so in the community... well, in Madrid it's already declared a cultural activity, whereupon the state will subsidise it, or will lower the taxes so the show goes well. So I think that it's totally impossible to happen.

Do you think that bullfighting is cruel?

The bull, that if there were no bullfighting, wouldn't exist, currently now lives, as I said, in a very ample zone, and lives very well. For four years, the bull lives in a wide, extensive field, and the bull is alive for bullfighting.

About the bull suffering, technically it's been demonstrated it doesn't suffer, it's the same as for a boxer; while boxing, there's no pain. If the boxer suffers, he would run away from the ring. There are several studies that have proven the bull doesn't suffer. Regarding the bull's death, we should think about the anti-taurinos. Seems they are subsidized by American companies, big companies that produce dog and cat food. So here in Spain, I've no idea about other countries, but in Spain, those companies are paying people who are fond of bulls, which I've seen in the bullrings, they are placing some posters against the bullfight, but it's only because they are earning money, they have been paid!

And in Spain specifically, we take so much care of the animals, but we don't worry about hundreds of homeless people, sleeping on the streets, covered just with cardboard, or within a telephone booth or many other weird places. Nobody cares about that, Mr Zapatero, the president, most care more about the puppy, and the bulls and the rest of the animals. But all people like to eat a tasty steak, forgetting that an animal was killed for it, or a savoury fish, that is another animal being killed, that was living happily in the sea, in its natural environment, and has been fished and died suffocating. Nobody remembers that, but bullfighting? Why? Because there are economic interests, paid by an American company, as far as it seems, that produces dog food.

If the bull didn't die in the bullring, if it wasn't killed, then it may be a drama, but the show wouldn't be the same, and the bull will suffer more, then the bull will really feel pain; why? Because the bull in the heat of the moment doesn't suffer, if instead it wasn't killed, but later, it will really suffer for that is the time when it has cooled off. That wouldn't occur if it were killed in the show, that is what I think. And technically, it has been demonstrated the bull doesn't suffer, if it were suffering the bull would run away. It has been tested in the open field where a bull has been run within a *tienta* bullring, then the bull was released and it continued trying to charge, then they used the horse, the picador, and the bull went for it, being hurt by the spike. If the bull suffered, it would have gone into the field. Of course there are a few not brave enough that *will* run away, but no more than one or two out of a hundred.

I repeat again, with the anti-taurinos. I have a friend that used to work in a bus company, he was a driver, and he used to go to the bullring in Benalmádena every Sunday bringing tourists with him. Then, on his holiday week he went to the bullring with his family. Now it seems that he's the leader of the anti-taurinos in Malaga! You know why? Because there is a lot of unemployment, and not too many jobs, and he got paid for doing that, then that's the anti-taurino reality!

Do you think the ban will spread across Spain?

In Andalusia the ban won't happen. I mean, the bullfighting show will continue and I'm very calm about that, because I remember when I was eight or nine years old, I had the dream to be a bullfighter; there were some newspapers I read saying that in ten or fifteen years the bullfighting show will end, for several reasons. That has always been said, but the bullfighting festival is huge, ingrained in many taurine countries. In France it has been started recently and fans have increased a lot; in Mexico, Colombia, Venezuela, Peru; a great number of countries. I'm not really worried about it, in Andalusia that won't happen, I'm absolutely sure, it's impossible.

Equanimal

The Bull and The Ban

Rafael and Coral are activists in Madrid's foremost animal rights group, Equanimal. I went to visit them at their central office. I had watched their naked protests outside Las Ventas, Madrid's premium bullring, which was televised on news stations worldwide. Rafael and Coral are friendly, quiet, calm vegans in a smart and organised office, happy to counter any comments about misgivings and clichés about anti-bullfighting activism.

Rafael

Any animal breeder knows, in the milk industry, that little calves are taken away from their mothers; their mothers are calling them for hours, or even for days, they are calling for the children, they want the children back, also the children, the little calves are calling for their mothers, desperately seeking their mothers, calling them, and this is very traumatic for them for mothers and children alike. So it's very, very good proof that calves and mamas feel emotions; they feel loneliness, they feel fear, they feel love, and what is stronger than the love between mother and child? You can see it in the milk industry, you can see it if you live in the country, you can watch that, anybody can watch that, how mothers are calling to their children. Anyway, cows, like mamas of dogs or cats, anyone who has dogs or cats living with them, they know that they feel alone, they feel well, they feel bad, they are depressed, they have stress, they have anxiety, they are feeling funny, experience a whole range of emotions, so if this is the case of cats or a dog, it the same for a cow, it's no difference, of course with a pig or any other animals that we are using.

The Bull and The Ban

Why do you think it is that people differentiate between a dog and a cat and pets, and cows and pigs?

Rafael
It's a cultural difference, we are being grown up (*sic*), you see, and the idea that some animals are companions, like the pets, what you *call* pets, cats, dogs and whatever, and to be food, like cows and pigs whatever, it's completely cultural. If you grow up with a cow, you will experience love and feelings with that cow, with a pig, with a hen, with any animals people are normally eating. It's just cultural, because for example in China people are eating dogs and cats, they are eating them, they are killing them, eating them in restaurants, or even in some Asiatic countries they are eating monkeys. To eat a cat or a dog or a monkey here in Europe is barbaric, but it's completely the same, it's a cultural thing; it's nothing else.

Coral
What really happens is that the use of the animal is different, it means unfortunately that many people have animals as pets, cats and dogs, they use them as a companion, and at some point they get tired of them: leave them, or beat them until they are dead or similar. What I really want to say is that perhaps what is different, not in all the cases of course, is the usage, but the consideration is the same, as *objects to use.* You use a few as food, and another one as a companion, whenever you want. As to the act in fact of bullfighting, people arguing it is a good life for the bull, I think it won't justify in any case the murder. I mean, it's not because they have a great life, that it's justified that then you torture

154

and kill them in a *plaza* for the entertainment of a few. Also, those bulls *don't* live in freedom, they grow up for *that*, and their "good life" is from the human point of view; maybe those bulls don't think the same, and for sure they don't want to die the way they die. And about the fact it's a sudden death with a cut in the spinal cord; in many cases that's not true and then the death is slow and painful, apart from the previous agony of the whole show, and for me, that's not justified at all.

Rafael
To kill a bull is very difficult, a 500 or 600 kilo animal; to kill such a big and strong animal like the bull is very difficult, in the bullfighting ring very often the animal, the bull, is taken away and he's still alive, because it's really very difficult to kill an animal like that. This means that before killing him, he's being tortured in many ways, with lots of knives and the banderillas and all the things, the picador with the lance and what they are doing, like cutting the neck here (signals his neck at the back); all the things the bull has to go through is a big torture and a big pain for the animal because it's very difficult to kill him. So the question about whether bulls have better life than other animals is not the point; to kill someone and to torture someone is not acceptable in any way, of course in the slaughterhouses the animals are killed in an even more horrible way and this is why we are against that too, and this is why we consider both as unacceptable. The bullfighting is the same, unacceptable, because it's the torturing and killing of an animal, of a sentient being: it's not the point he's suffering less or suffering more, has a better life, or not such a good life, a little better life, a little worse; this is not the point, we are against slavery in

all its ways. Just consider that you have slaves, human slaves, you can have human slaves with a good life, they have all the commodities, big rooms, they have whatever – Internet access, they have food – or you have slaves in very bad conditions, many people in the same room, almost no food. Of course that is worse, but slavery is not good in any case, whether the slaves are well treated or not so well treated, so it's the same here, we are against the use of individuals against the rule; we don't mind if life is better or life is worse, and of course we are against the killing of animals for food the same as we are against bullfighting.

Coral
About the animal holocaust; the amount of animals that die daily for the food industry is enormous, holocaustic proportions in fact, while the amount of bulls dying is much less that the animals killed for the food industry. The quantity is not relevant, each animal is important, even if it's only one it's justified.

Rafael
I don't think it is a "good death". First of all I *don't want* to be killed, first slow or fast, no one wants to be killed, no individual wants to be killed, where it's a quick death or slow death, of course if I'm going to be killed I prefer a quick death of course, but in the first case I don't want to be killed – so a bull is the same. Second, the bull doesn't suffer normally a quick death, because it is very difficult to kill a 500 or 600 kilogram animal, it's very difficult, it's a very strong animal, and I've seen bullfighting, I've seen, I've been there, as I said before, and you see the animal suffering, going around, tumbling down, going to the

floor, getting up again, and all the stupid *toreros* around pushing him, it lasts, it takes time, and sometimes the bull is being taken away from the *plaza* and he's still alive, he cannot move because his spinal cord is cut, he cannot move but he *feels*, this is something that happens, you cannot move because here is cut but you can feel. And there after the bull is being butchered alive, the bull is being cut into pieces, and he still feels. I don't think... sometimes maybe it's a quick death but very often it's not, and you can see that, you can watch a bullfight and you'll see that, it's very difficult to kill that animal.

Coral
What you just commented on, I think it shows a relevant thing, that the bull needs extraordinary stimulation to attack, that shows what it really is, a mammal, a ruminant, that what he likes is being in the field grazing on grass, that he may attack others only if he feels it's attacked, if he sees danger, if he has to defend young or the herd. The fighting bull is a fake, that his objective in life is to attack the bullfighters or fight in the *plaza* for his life, that is false, they are ruminant and what they like is being in the field eating grass; that's why there's a need to stick in the banderillas, to torture him, to massacre him so he attacks because what he really wants is to get away from there, is get rid of the pain.

Rafael
There is something else, and that is the bull is an animal that normally doesn't make any sound; they don't make sounds. In the bullfighting you can hear them crying, they are crying, and they are not crying because they are feeling pain; when they cry it's because they are warning

the others in case there are other bulls in the area saying "Careful, here is danger, here they are attacking me, they are killing me, go away!" He's warning others, other bulls in the area to go away, to escape from there because there is danger. Many people they don't know, they think the bull is crying because he's feeling pain, the bull normally... bulls don't cry because they are very strong animals, they cry because they are telling others to go away, to fly, to fly away from danger.

Coral
In fact in many situations bulls have been seen jumping into the crowd, going outside of the bullring with the intent of escaping, to escape from pain. It's completely false they want to be there fighting, it is not true, and it's completely demonstrated.

Rafael
Bulls are not aggressive animals, they are pacific animals; when they are being grown up, people who are taking care of them, they go to them in their cars, it's no problem, they are not aggressive, they only attack in the bullfight arena because they are being provoked and they are being tortured, they are being hurt and they react there, they are fighting for their lives, they are just fighting for their lives, not aggressive animals at all; the people in the bullfight want to make us believe that they are aggressive animals. Only carnivorous animals are aggressive, but not herbivores such as bulls, they are not aggressive at all.

Don't you think the banning of bullfighting is going to have an effect on Spain's culture?

The Bull and The Ban

Rafael

You know in Spain there has been a controversy in the animal rights movement, whether to fight against bullfighting or not, because bullfighting is a very little area of animal abuse actually, only just some thousands of animals against the millions and millions of animals who are being killed in other areas like for food or experimentation, why we are fighting against bullfighting? Because it's very symbolic; the bullfight is actually and unfortunately the symbol of Spain, of the Spanish culture, unluckily many people around the world when they think about Spain they think about bullfighting, it's something very disgusting for us Spaniards, but this is what it is, you go to Japan, you go to China, you go to USA, and "Ah Spain, bullfighting!". It's like a symbol of our country, how are you going to fight for animal rights in a country whose main symbol, main character is an animal being tortured, an animal being killed? It's very symbolic of the Spanish culture, and this is why we are fighting against that, because when we finish with bullfighting we'll only finish with a little area of animal abuse but a big area of animal abuse in our minds.

Coral

What would happen if the bullfighting finishes, traditions and culture of the society, in this case the Spanish one, may suffer a reduction of its idiosyncrasy. And about what would happen if the bullfighting finishes, if we will experiment with a cultural reduction, in tradition, etc. Well, when for example, in the Middle Ages people stopped carrying out public executions, witch burning, or many other multiple examples, but that could happen too then, they could also think that part of the tradition and culture would be lost and that it could be terrible. Obviously I think that tradition and culture in general have to be reviewed, you have to go forward, and if something we do now is considered bad and we can't justify it from any point of view, ethical or moral, we must stop it, we have to let it go and continue with something else, something better, something that makes us better, something that makes our culture richer, for our fiestas and traditions.

Rafael
Well I think that society is not a static thing, society is a dynamic thing, it's always moving, it's like a river where you never see the same water, so society is always evolving and of course if you end up with a tradition, this tradition will not come back and you'll have a change in the society, but society is always changing anyway, so as Coral said very well, we end up with traditions which are not with the spirit of the time anymore. For example in this country, in Spain, it was a tradition to burn people alive, with the Inquisition, it was a very nice tradition we had some hundred years ago but luckily we don't have it any more; traditions appear and traditions finish, it's how it is because the world is moving on, and you can move on with the world, you can move on with the time, or you can remain static and don't evolve and remain with your past. It's the same as people who don't evolve with their lives; they are always attached to their past, to the other spirits they had in the past, you have to evolve as a person. The same as a person, a society has to evolve, and I think that to end up with a tradition is not good, is not bad, is something which happens, traditions start and traditions finish, and in this case it is a tradition which

means suffering, which mean a killing of individuals, so the same as other traditions that we finished, this one has to finish too, and this is not going to be bad for society, because society will change anyway and hopefully what we want is that the changes are for good, not for bad.

What do you think when people say you know nothing about bullfighting and you have no arguments, and that you, as animal activists, are unreasonable people? One torero describes you and your methods as sinister and dangerous...

Coral
It's not true, I think it's not true what is said, I think that at least we try, we have scientific support, we give backed arguments, as Rafael said, by ethnologists, zoologists; we try to give answers to all questions that people coming to us may require. We promote the debate. I don't think it's true we don't have arguments and we don't provide a believable explanation, it's not true at all. And about the methods, I understand some protests may be liked or not from a few, but it's what we said before, what we really try is the best method to communicate to most people; we want people to hear us. To go out with a banner has a minor impact in society; people are tired of common manifestations and almost nobody pays attention to what is said; a manifestation can pass in front of you and you won't even pay attention, you don't even know what they are saying and perhaps it's an interesting issue for you. So we look for other methods, methods calling people's attention; if it's annoying to see some people naked, that's not

understandable either, there's a symbolic issue, the nudity itself; we are also animals, and animals go naked, why can't we be naked? What's the problem with that? I think they are cultural matters, a few good, a few bad. To torture an animal is right, but a naked person protesting is not? It doesn't make sense, and doesn't have any value.

Rafael

In Britain, and the animal rights movement across Europe, there are many people involved in the animal rights movement; this means all kinds of people, this is a social fight, this *is* a fight, this is a struggle for a better world; you cannot expect that a fight doesn't have... how to say, not violence, but conflict; so a confrontation. There's always confrontation. We are fighting against people who are abusing, torturing and killing animals. Never forget that every second that passes, every moment I'm speaking, three thousand animals are being killed, this is an estimation with all the statistics we have of animals used in the world, every second three thousand animals are being killed in the world. This is not a joke, this is not a game, not a minor thing; it is very important. Millions and millions of animals are being killed every moment in the world for any reason; for food, for entertainment, for experimentation, whatever, so it is an important fight. People who say we are using shocking ways of calling attention, attracting attention; Yes, we do, of course we have to use shocking ways of calling attention so people are looking at us and people think about us. The naked protest has shown that people have come to think about bullfighting, have come to think about the idea of using animals. We must provoke, we must do provoking things to call attention, if we don't they are just going to ignore us, because it's not something that has to do with their lives, it has to do with the lives of others, of the animals, and they are not animals so it's not their problem. If we are not doing shocking things, provoking things, people are not going to pay any attention to us. About what you say, we are not reasonable, well it's their opinion. Of course anybody can talk to me or to Coral, or to any animal right activist, and we can talk to anyone; my arguments are solid because I speak in the name of ethics, in the name of non-violence. I'm speaking in the name of respect; I can talk to anyone, I don't have any problem to talk to anyone, a bullfighter, a hunter, a dissectionist (*sic*), whoever; I can talk to them, because I have arguments and my arguments are respectful for anyone who can feel, these are my arguments. I can talk to anyone, the same as me, as she, and any other animal right activist. We can talk to anyone, it's not that we are not reasonable, it's that maybe they don't want to hear us; this may be the point.

Coral shows me their most "sinister" weapon for protest, a cuddly bull costume complete with head and horns.

Coral
For example, at Bio Culture, Madrid's bio culture fair, we have used him there; we use him in the same way as in other activities, to call attention, especially for young people. I'll wear it now if I can, he's called Teddy! Here there are the legs, the hooves, does it fit alright?! *(Wears the costume and head)*

163

Rafael
This has been taken to demonstrations, it's very good for little children because little children talk to him and say "Oh Mummy, there's a big bull there!" And then they talk to us, it's very good.

(Rafael shows me around the office.) And what is this poster here? (A poster of an elephant and a monkey)

Rafael
It's about animal liberation in general; it's all different horrible things we are doing to our companions, and why we are against that.

And what are the boxes you've got here in the office?

Rafael
There are many things, t-shirts mostly; posters, merchandising things, whatever, we have here a lot of material. Hopefully there's no bullfighter coming here to set fire to it all!

Graham Bell

Graham is a friend of mine who is an eco-artist who lives in the neighbouring province to Catalonia, Valencia. He explores the concept that we are animals, and nature is part of who we are. Originally from Scotland, he now speaks fluent Spanish and is often featured in the news and current affairs programmes in Spain as well as the press. I wanted to ask him about the ecological issues of meat production and the issue of killing animals for food. What is the dilemma, and why is he vegetarian? Why is vegetarianism so rare in Spain? And as a foreigner, what are his views on bullfighting?

Do you think bullfighting is cruel?

I've been living in Spain for about six years now and I've been only to one bullfight, which was a beginner's bullfight, as they call it. I left before they finished because there seemed to be so many men involved in the killing of this bull that it didn't really seem to be the one-on-one valiant kind of courageous fight that I had envisaged.

As a vegetarian, and as a Scot, I feel I don't necessarily have the opinion to criticise other people's traditions, but, well, obviously I have my own point of view as a vegetarian. I think that animals should be respected, and that keeping animals for food or any other purpose is inhumane really.

So that's my personal opinion, obviously I live in Spain and respect other people's opinions but I hope that soon the attitudes will change and things will become easier, not only for the bull, but for the vegetarians who unfortunately seem to be in the minority! In the UK, there are lot more vegetarians and there is a different way of looking at animals and animal cruelty.

What are the differences you've found?

I suppose the main difference between the UK and Spain when it comes to animal rights is that people are more aware in Britain and consider that it's an injustice. Originally, I thought that the reason that there wasn't such awareness here was that the animals were actually kept in much better conditions in Spain but now I'm not so sure. I think factory farming is now a universal practise so I don't believe in the kind of free-range thing that I used to believe. I think it's actually very difficult to explain why there are more vegetarians in Britain than Spain; I'm not really sure why that is. There are so many cultural differences, but in general I think the attitude towards nature in Britain is much more respectful because I suppose of the industrial revolution we have a different history and we have more of a nostalgia for the beauty of nature and animals.

Something which hasn't really happened in Spain because the industrial revolution's never really had a great affect outside of the Basque Country, where of course bullfighting is not practised, and Catalonia, where they are very much against it. You see, across Spain the kind of differences also affected by the effects of the industrial revolution and practices and ways of seeing Nature versus Culture.

Do you think that, in the UK, there is a much bigger consumer culture than in Spain? Do you think that Spanish culture is more of a production society?

I think that it's true in Britain that there is more of a demand and supply kind of connection, where if somebody sees that there is a gap in the market for vegetarian food then they will fill it. There's probably a huge gap in the market in Spain for vegetarian food but it's actually impossible to find. In huge hypermarkets here you can find food from the Philippines, anywhere around the world, but there will not even be a section of vegetarian food, so it's actually a little bit bizarre for some of us who live here. Although, in the end, it takes you back to the early days of vegetarianism where you prepare your own food and in some ways it's more natural than the kind of 'junk' vegetarian food you can get in Britain, which I used to eat more. So the consumer aspect is an important part of that.

Why did you become a vegetarian?

Well, I grew up on a farm, so I'm not particularly sentimental about animals and killing animals because all animals kill other animals to survive.

The main reason I became a vegetarian was to do with land use and the fact that it's a waste to feed up a cow on a stretch of land that could feed so many more people. And that was really one of the main reasons I became a vegetarian. I do think that animals should be free. For example, I visit friends in Scotland who live in the countryside and if they have shot a deer or they have killed an animal, which has lived in a natural environment I would eat it, so I'm not a strict vegetarian, but I am against the use of land and the cruelty involved in agricultural practices that are in use today.

Can you tell me about the eco-art projects that you do?

I recently was a curator for an exhibition about ecology and gender, which was about performance, gender, natural and unnatural behaviours. The show was heavily influenced by the work of Annie Sprinkle and her work on eco-sexuality and later by practices of eco-feminism, which I was interested in. It touched on themes of how humans see animals, and how animals see humans really too. The gender roles of masculine and feminine are seen as the different ways that we perform and this exhibition was actually to try and open up the idea that, as we are animals, perhaps we can all see another aspect to the human behaviour which would be more in tune with our natural environment if we were to learn from animals and how they behave, how they treat and respect their own environment and don't turn it into a trash can!

Jason Webster

Jason Webster's books were my first foray into really seriously reading about Spain. "Duende", "Sacred Sierra" and "Andalus" are about his travels as a young man into flamenco, bullfighting and the reality of living in Spain. I read him alongside Hemingway and Lewine, and his were the books I read on the coach when emigrating. I was keen to interview him about his opinions as a Brit now living in Spain, but also to get into some deeper thoughts into why bullfighting is so important to so many people. I was thrilled with the interview he gave in the very room he writes his books in. I think I was a bit of a fan girl, but he was gracious and kind, even coming to find us when we got completely lost in a dodgy part of town. His new series of fiction, the Max Cámara Novels, start with "Or The Bull Kills You", a gritty detective novel about a murdered bullfighter in Valencia.

As a foreigner, what's the most difficult aspect to understand about bullfighting?

Well, I suppose it's the public slaughter of a bull, of an animal on a stage like that. When I've spoken to English people, Americans and foreigners about bullfighting, that's often the thing that they'll say to me, that they'll talk about, they'll say it's making killing some form of entertainment.

But I think that's where they're making the mistake because I don't think bullfighting is entertainment. I don't think it's really seen as an entertainment here. It's not a sport, that's obviously a mistake that a lot of foreign commentators might make about bullfighting, they talk about it as a sport, in the same way that other people might go and watch a game of football or baseball or whatever at the weekend. So it doesn't take place every weekend, it's not a sport. The reports for a bullfight are on the same pages as the ballet reports or the opera reports in the Spanish newspapers, so it's an art, it's a performance art, and it's a ritual. It's a sort of quasi-religious sacred ritual. So these are things I think which help to understand perhaps what bullfighting is, and therefore come to terms possibly with the whole concept of a public killing, a killing that's done in front of a live audience, which makes it look like entertainment, but as I say, it isn't really.

Do you think there's a difference between the definition of art, in say western European culture, to the definition of art within this area of the world?

That's such a difficult question, because, art; how does one define art? There's an endless debate about that. And I can't really get into that now, but, if you say, "Bullfighting is art, so therefore it's OK", Well, on the surface that's a pretty meaningless statement, it's like saying we could turn anything into art, we could say anything is art and then therefore it's fine. We could say killing a human being is art, and that obviously doesn't work. Is there some kind of art in bullfighting? Yes, I think so. I think, because, it's not just the pageantry, obviously there is a lot of pageantry, there's a lot of costume, it's a three act play, each killing of the bull is like a three act play. I mean, these are obvious examples, which make it like a drama and an art in that sense. But I think if you see a bullfight where something exceptional happens, and I have maybe twice, two or three times, that's when you can say, I think you can start saying, "Yes, there is something".

There's a more powerful concept of art that suddenly enters into the equation at this point. What is this moment? Well, it's not easy to describe or even to explain, you might say that it's a *duende* moment. Similar to the duende moments that you get in *flamenco*. It's the moments when the hair stands up on the back of your neck; something special seems to be happening, something magical. So, if you're alive to that, if you can sense that, and you are present when it takes place, then I think bullfighting becomes something transformative. There's a transformative power to it, and it transcends the mere act of a man killing a bull. It becomes something else. What does it become? Well, I don't know. Perhaps I have an idea, but we're getting into realms where words can't really help us out. It's something that you have to feel.

You've often spoken in your books about, maybe in Britain in particular, that there's some kind of – I'm paraphrasing – some kind of stunted emotional thing that happens with British people, that you then come to Spain and you can open up more. Do you think that could have something to do with the misunderstanding of the moment of duende in bullfighting that people chase here, that you don't really understand it in Britain maybe because there's that dislocation?

Possibly. There's a general trend of British people coming down to the Mediterranean, it might be Spain, it might be

Italy, it might be other Mediterranean countries, and sort of finding something. They feel more relaxed, they feel more natural, they find some sort of spiritual home perhaps, a place where they can be themselves more than in the traditional repressed kind of society we have in Britain. I don't think it is quite so much these days; obviously E.M Forster is a classic example of this, in his case it was Italy.

What I think the Spanish are very good at, and that we're not very good at, for example, in Britain, is they are socially very intelligent. It's very difficult in Spain to be atomised, to use Welbeck's famous phrase. It's a country where the moment you walk out into the street, people are greeting you, they're saying hello, you go into a shop, you get a low level amount of attention and social interaction just walking around. And this I think reflects some kind of greater emotional intelligence than we might have in British society. How does this relate to bullfighting? I think that what the Spanish are good at, they understand that we have to look after certain aspects of what it is to be human: the social side of being human, the emotional side of being human, and possibly an aggressive or a violent or a primitive, if you want to use that word, side of being a human being, and that is possible what you will see in bullfighting.

What really interests me about bullfighting is the roots, the origins of bullfighting. It looks as though bullfighting maybe some kind of a remnant of an old Bronze Age fertility ritual. If you go back and you look at old cave paintings, you often see bulls, I mean, bulls throughout the Mediterranean are big – they're a very powerful image. We obviously know about the Minoan culture and the bull jumping and the acrobatics they used to do, but bull worship of some sort was taking place all over the Mediterranean.

And often in some of the old cave paintings you see the bull represented with a solar disk in between his two horns. So the bull is somehow, in most of these Mediterranean cultures, he's somehow representing the sun, he's representing fertility, and it's about the growing of crops and basically, you know, staying alive. And some of this you can see reflected in modern day bullfighting. Bullrings are round, like the sun, and the bull comes in from the East gate, like the rising of the sun. So there are all these echoes of a tradition which stretches back thousands of years. Now, what's possibly taking place in a bullfight is that you've got this very powerful sexual imagery, erotic imagery, being played out. It's a drama, it's a sexual and lethal, a life and death, struggle, that's being played out in front of an audience. And there's a kind of blood lust thing taking place there. So if you go to a bullfight, often what I've found afterwards, if it's been a good bullfight – I mean, most bullfights are bad, it has to be said, and when you see a bad bullfight, it's just a man killing a bull and it's not attractive; it's very bloody and it's very messy – when you see a good bullfight, it starts having some other quality to it. And you come away and you actually feel strangely cleansed, you feel strangely more relaxed and you feel different. And this is what I mean about why I think the Spanish have certain kinds of intelligence that we don't really have in Britain. And this may be one of them, where they understand that we are

primitive animals as well as being intellectual, whatever it
is.

There is a primitive side to us and for thousands of years
human societies have had some kind of blood ritual built
in to the structure of their society, which has kind of
channelled, somehow dealt with this killing, bloodlust
instinct that we probably all have inside us. And it may
have been through warfare; obviously the Romans had
their circuses – but some kind of blood ritual seems to
have been present in many human societies throughout
human history, until today and in modern society we just
don't have that. We're meant to just sit in offices and
work on our computers and pay our taxes and pay our
mortgages, and then, you know, that's it. That's your life.
So I think, where do so many frustrations come in from
modern life, from modern living? Well perhaps because
we are not looking after certain needs that we have. Our
social needs, our emotional needs, and maybe a
bloodlust need, and that is I think possibly something
that's taking place with the bullfights in Spain, and that's
an example of where the Spanish are more intelligent
than British or Anglo-Saxon society.

*So what do you think about the trend for vegetarianism in
Britain, which is on the increase, and the perceived
activism against bullfighting with celebrities in the USA
and the UK at the moment?*

I have total respect for vegetarians who are against
bullfighting because I think that is entirely logical. I think
that if you eat meat and you wear leather shoes and have
leather handbags, you have to square that circle. Why is

that alright? Why is it alright to slaughter millions and *millions* of cows, in this case, bulls, in abattoirs in these sort of industrialised factories of death that we have created? Why is that alright, but it's not alright for a few thousand bulls to be killed in Spanish bullfighting culture and in Latin American bullfighting culture? So, I think you have to answer that question.

Some people may say "Well, it's because it's done in public", which to me is a further argument in favour of not banning bullfighting. It's not hypocritical. So why are we saying that it's okay to be hypocritical about killing animals? So as long as we don't see it, as long as I just go to the supermarket and I see my nicely packaged piece of meat there in its little plastic box, that's alright, but I don't want to see how it came here, I don't want to see what happened for me to have that piece of meat or for me to have my leather shoes. "Please remove all the goriness". It's like children, really, I find it slightly childish, that attitude, because it's saying, you know, "Mummy Mummy, please take away the nastiness".

I think for a vegetarian to be against bullfighting is totally logical and it's a position I respect. I'm not a vegetarian. I eat meat, so it seems to me that it would feel hypocritical to be against bullfighting. That said, I mean, I obviously have mixed feelings about bullfighting. It's not something that I think one should approach with a black and white frame of mind. A lot of people have that black and white thing about bullfighting, "It's just terrible, so we need to get rid of it" or "It's just wonderful, it's a tradition and we have to preserve it". I think it's much more complicated, much more complex than that. And that's partly what I try to do in my book about bullfighting, is explore these grey areas, these moral grey areas, and they are huge and they're there to be explored I think if you're interested in this. But you do have to answer these questions.

We are slightly strange in Britain about animals. I don't know if people in Britain understand or see how strange they are, seen from outside, because we are incredibly protective about our animals, but we still eat them. So it's okay to have your fillet of steak, but don't touch my bunny rabbit, and I've got posters of kittens all over the walls.

We've anthropomorphised animals to such an extent through whatever, Walt Disney films are a perfect example, that I think a lot of people might see a bull in a bullring and it's as though they're seeing a human being, and they're almost seeing themselves there. They're identifying with the bull, not with the man, which is quite strange if you think about it. Why identify with a bull? In most cases, you eat steaks – you don't identify with the cow that you're eating, but when you see it taking place in the arena, you identify with the bull rather than the bullfighter. The bullfighter is the baddie and the bull is the goodie and the victim and we're on his side. Obviously, Spanish people don't see it like that at all. They're looking at the bull because they're not there just to see the bull get killed, they want to see a powerful bull, they want to see a bravo bull, they want to see a bull that's going to take the fight to the bullfighter. It's about the two coming together and fighting, and somehow welding, turning into one. That's obviously the ideal bullfight – is when bullfighter and bull sort of merge into one being.

I'm sort of digressing here. But it's something much more complex, much more powerful; it has deep, deep roots as I say, probably going back to the Bronze Age. And to just come along in our mechanised modern world where we don't want any gore and we don't want to see any nastiness and to start saying, "Oh we've got to get rid of this, it's terrible!" Well, you know, I just think that's a little bit silly.

Do you think that people outside of Spain have a right to enter this debate?

Sure, absolutely, I mean, otherwise, if you said they didn't have the right to enter into the debate, you could say that in the 1930s and '40s, nobody had the right to enter into the debate as to whether Germany should treat its Jews in the way that it did, so you can't say nobody outside Spain should not get involved in this debate. It's a moral debate. It's something which affects all human beings. But I think if you want to enter into the debate, you should understand what you are talking about. You should learn about bullfighting. And certainly criticise it, of course. But find out what you're talking about. Don't just look at it from a distance and say, "Oh that's terrible, and I don't want anything to do with it." That's a sort of Mary Whitehouse attitude, you know, "I didn't see Romans in Britain, but I heard it was terrible, let's ban it". And this is another thing, I mean, we live in a strange time where it's like we just feel that anything we don't like we should ban.

Again this is another reason why I find it hard to say whether I'm pro-bullfighting or against bullfighting. I think I can say for certain that I am against anti-bullfighting. (Laughs) That's as clear as mud, I suppose. But, yes, there's this strange thing where we just want to ban things that we don't like. It's a curious aspect of our current society.

Hemingway was criticised in the '30s in one particular article for glamorising bullfighting as a foreigner, writing about bullfighting and glamorising it, and the opinion of the journalist that wrote about it was that he didn't really have the right to write about it because he's a foreigner. How do you feel about that when you're writing about it?

I'm certainly not trying to glamorise it. I'm trying to understand it. I mean, what I've done in my novel, it's a detective novel, it's a murder. It involves a murder of Spain's greatest bullfighter, and the detective who is investigating this murder is a member of the Spanish police force and he, like the majority or Spaniards, he doesn't like bullfighting. He's not interested in it. So I was interested in that development. How does a policeman who doesn't like bullfighting, how does he investigate the murder of a bullfighter? A bullfighter to him is just somebody who goes around killing animals and is little better than a murderer himself, so there's an immediate moral tension there, that's what I was interested in, and also it was a way in to firstly talk about aspects of bullfighting, explain aspects of bullfighting, as he is himself learning about it. And secondly, to explore these grey areas. Explore the grey area that, bullfighting for me, sits right in; it's neither black nor white. It's in this curious moral grey zone, and you can explore that and wend your way through it and say, "What about this? What about that? What about such and such?" I think as a writer you have to, in certain situations, I think it's sort of your duty almost to look at these grey areas when everyone else is looking at a topic in black and white terms.

Have you got anything to say about the Catalonia situation?

I think it's partly to do with Catalonia trying to express itself as an independent region, as not part of the rest of Spain. I think they're doing so in a strange way because there has always been a strong tradition of bullfighting in Catalonia. I think, for my tupenny-ha'penny's worth, is that they're going about it in the wrong way. To get rid of bullfighting is sort of playing to the public; they're sort of doing it to the rest of the world; I think there's an element of that. I think there's an element of saying, "Look, we Catalans are a bit more sophisticated and a bit better. We're better people than the other Spaniards, because they go around killing bulls". Sort of forgetting that they have this long tradition of bullfighting and that they haven't banned the bull running which takes place in Catalonia.

Again we're sort of entering into this strange hypocritical area where it's like "You can do this, but you can't do that". Well, why is it okay to ban bullfighting but not to get rid of bull running, which is a huge part of the fiestas in the towns of southern Catalonia and Tarragona, where they have bulls running with the flames where they put these torches on the bull's horns at night, and it's very spectacular but I don't think the bull's having a great time! And they're running around and they're just charging at all the kids and all the people who want to run with the bull. So, why do one and not do the other? I think there are questions there that need to be answered and I don't think they have answered them.

I don't think it will go any further. I don't think any other region in Spain will ban bullfighting. At least not for the next twenty years. I think it's interesting that five or six years ago, bullfighting was probably closer to dying or being on its knees in Spain than it is now. And it's now probably healthy for two reasons: one because of a bullfighter called José Tomás who came back from retirement and is an example of the best kind of a bullfighter, who really puts his life on the line every single time and is an exceptional matador, one of the best in the history of bullfighting. I think that's generally agreed. So he has kind of vivified bullfighting again. And secondly, because of the Catalan ban. I think in the rest of Spain they've realised that bullfighting could be under threat, and that they need to look after it and protect it as part of their cultural heritage. So in many ways you could say that the Catalan ban has put back the possibility of banning bullfighting by another twenty years.

Do you think that the age of celebrity has a lot to do with this, almost, rebirth of the heroes of the ring?

That's an interesting question. I think that one of the really interesting things about bullfighting is that, with a bullfighter, that's about as close as we can get in the twenty-first century to the old monster slayers of the mythological age. Where else can you go where you can say, "I met this guy and he slays monsters"? You know, that's incredible. It's like saying, "I went back in time and I spoke to Theseus".

So, there is this link, I think, between bullfighting and this ancient world. We're talking about Bronze Age, perhaps even older. We're actually tapping into a pre-patriarchal society. We're going back to an old matriarchal society. It's that old. And for me, I'm interested in history, I'm interested in archaeology, I'm interested in myths and stories; so for me, bullfighting envelops all of this in many ways. And it has an extra interest, an extra fascination. So, going back to your question of current celebrity culture, and how does that influence the way bullfighting is going. Bullfighters have always been celebrities, but in the real sense because they're guys who actually do something, they really do something, and they really do put their lives on the line. Don't let anybody ever tell you that bullfighting is easy. Yes, there is corruption in bullfighting. Yes, there are cases of bulls being doped. And there is a dark side to bullfighting, a dodgy side to bullfighting, which any true bullfighting aficionado would scorn. It does take place, but on the whole, a bullfighter stepping out into the ring is really putting his life on the line, and that's true.

So when you meet a bullfighter, you're talking to a man who has faced death many times, and that's not easy to find in our day and age, and that's very interesting, to talk to somebody who has many, many times looked death in the face.

The Bull and The Ban

Glossary

Words used in this book are given meanings here, so that readers may grasp the issues. They are listed here in outline and are not intended to be encyclopaedic knowledge, just a broad stroke for those not privy to bullfighting or Spanish language.

Aficionado/a – A fan of bullfighting, with "afición" or a passion for taurine activities.

Anti-taurino – Animal rights activist or person outspoken against bullfighting.

Ayuda – Helper, assistant. Also the fake wooden sword used in the first part of the *tercio de muerte* (See Tercio) before the kill.

Banderilla – (Literally "Little Flag") The barbed, flag-coloured sticks used to prick the bull. Often in the colours of Spain's yellow and red flag, or Andalusia's green and white, but it seems different rules apply per region and flags from different regions are used according to either the matador's birthplace or the location of the bullring.

Banderillero – A man whose profession is to place the banderillas.

Bloodsport – An activity where a sport is carried out, such as in fox hunting, where riding horses is the sport and an animal is killed. Bullfighting is sometimes considered a bloodsport, but in fact there is no sport and therefore many consider bullfighting a cultural or artistic endeavour, not a sport.

Boletín – Form

Bravo – To describe a brave bull, "toro bravo" but also has a connection to trapio in that it is used during a bullfight to comment on his performance in the bullring.

Caballo – Horse

Callejon – The small alleyway between the bullring and the audience at a bullfight, marked with a series of wooden panels for the toreros to jump behind to protect themselves from the bull.

Campo – The countryside; used in bullfighting to describe a training or recce trip to a breeding ranch to cape some of the cows or calves for practice or training, or to view the earmarked stock for the upcoming season.

Capote – The cape used in the first part of the bullfight to slow the bull as it enters the ring. Usually magenta and yellow, but recently the yellow is replaced for fashion or charity purposes with blue or patterned faces.

Carnet Professional – Employment papers

Carretón – A bull's head mounted on a bicycle wheel used for training banderilleros and for capework in *toreo*.

Catalan – A person from Catalonia or the language of Catalonia (Català), the Balearics, Andorra, and the Roussillon region of France.

Catalonia – "Catalonia is an autonomous region of Spain in the north-east of the Iberian Peninsula, with the official status of a nationality. Catalonia comprises four provinces: Barcelona, Girona, Lleida, and Tarragona". (Wikipedia)

Catalonian – To be from Catalonia. Used less frequently to describe a Catalan person, more to describe anything to originate in Catalonia.

Comparecencia – Hearing, as in Parliament where an opinion is heard for the vote.

Correbous – A Catalan word for "running of the bulls/oxen", usually run in the street on a long tether to prevent escape, or into the sea and chased and taunted by the local people during fiestas.

Correfoc – A Catalan word for "Running of fire" where a bull has its horns set on fire and is run in the streets as above.

Correr – To run

Corrida de Toros – (Often referred to as "corrida") The bullfight itself, the running of the bull in Spanish.

Cuadrilla – The squad available to the matador during the bullfight.

Estoque de Descabello – Also called Descabello. Sword for killing the bull.

Faena – (Literally, "The Task") The last round of the bullfight when the bull will be drawn in with the muleta and killed with the sword in one blow to the neck. The name suggests the killing of the bull is not relished by the public or the matador.

Feria – Fair or festival usually held at the expense of the local council for the locals to enjoy at no expense, such as a fair and drinking tents with bands and dancing.

Fiesta Nacional – The National Festival, which is the bullfight itself.

Finca – Estate or farm, also used as a word for the ranches where bulls are bred.

ILP – The Initiative of Popular Legislation is similar to a white paper in UK politics, to be voted upon in Catalan Parliament. A submission of a petition/proposal for a change in the Catalan law.

Impresario – Business owner or promoter, usually of the bullring.

Indultado (or "indultao" in Andalusian dialect) – A bull who fights well and is excused from the bullfight, pardoned by the president/public (sometimes unofficially requested by the matador) during the corrida's last round, usually just before the kill, who is rounded up and sent back as stud to his ranch for the rest of his days.

Los toros – The bulls, also to mean the whole interest or hobby of bullfighting, or the festival time of bullfighting which generally runs from around April to October in Europe and continues in the Americas over the Winter.

Matador – A bullfighter who has trained and passed his exam, the alternativa, and killed a bull.

Mozo de Espadas – Literally the Sword Boy, but is usually a man who arranges all swords and capes for the matador, and dresses him. General concierge.

Muleta – (Literally "crutch") The red cape used at the end of a bullfight to draw the bull closer in for the kill.

Murilleros – Workers who drag the body of the bull from the ring with mules.

Murillo – Muscle on the back of the bull's neck.

Nazarenes – The brotherhoods that wear a pointed hat, mask and cape to parade the streets during Santa Semana to do penance. Often mistakenly thought that these costumes are Ku Klux Klan, but actually are ancient and nothing to do with it. The conical hat symbolises the rise to Heaven of Jesus, or the penitent, and the mask to aid solace.

Novillada – Student bullfight without a picador.

Novillero – Novice bullfighter.

Ole – Used to comment on the passes made by the matador during the last third of the corrida, but used softly and seriously for good passes. God help the Englishman who drunkenly cries out *Ole!* in the bullring! No translation to English as such, but according to Jason Webster in his book "Andalus" there could be some connection to the (Moorish) Arabic "Allah", meaning God or "By God", but also to my ears, the word "Oye!" ("Listen up") is used colloquially like, "Hey!" in the Andalusian dialect is almost identical in sound and meaning, and less mystical. A common remark in Andalusia when watching anything interesting and so in my opinion likely to have come from there.

Opus Dei – Spanish founded Catholic group of lay persons with secular priests. Literally, "Work of God". It has been alleged that Opus Dei had strong links to the Franco regime. Opus Dei was misrepresented in the film "Da Vinci Code" in 2006. However, Opus Dei does practice mortification of the flesh and celibacy and some members live in group housing.

Passes – The name given to a move of the cape in front of the bull during a bullfight. The most famous passes are The *Verónica* (A slow pass away from the bull named after Veronica who wiped a handkerchief across Jesus' brow in the Bible) and The Natural (A pass made with the left hand, much revered), but many more are created as time goes on.

Peon – One of the crew of the matador, literally "pawn" as in chess. A slightly derogatory term, to mean the lower ranks of workers.

Pic – A verb or noun used in English by Hemingway to describe the lance, or the action of the lance prick of the vara, now used commonly to speak about the picador. "Zurito sat there, his feet in the box stirrups, his great legs in the buckskin-covered armor . . . the reins in his left hand, the long pic held in his right hand, his broad hat well down over his eyes to shade them from the lights" The Undefeated, Ernest Hemingway, 1927.

Picador – A man whose profession it is to ride horseback into the bullring and prick the bull with a spear.

Plaza de Toros – (Often referred to as "Plaza") The bullring itself.

Prensa Rosa – (Literally, the "Pink Press") The gossip columns in Spain.

The Public – The audience at a bullfight are commonly known as "El Publico" as in the theatre.

Puya – Spike on the end of the lance used by the picador.

Puyazo – The act of spiking the bull with the puya.

Rejoneador – Bullfighter on horseback.

Santa Semana – Easter festival in Spain which follows Jesus and his crucifixion and rise from the dead, with many parades and penances.

Sorteo – The drawing of lots for the six bulls for three matadors. Done with straws or papers.

Suerte – The round of the bullfight ("Luck" in Spanish also).

Tapita – Small tapas, which is a snack size serving of food.

Taurina – A shortening of the more colloquial term, *"carretilla taurina"*. The *carretón*.

Taurino – A bullfighting afición or worker, or anything to do with bulls.

Tauromaquia – Everything to do with bullfighting and bulls, in particular the art and tradition.

Tentadero – The closed ring used for the tienta.

Tercio – There are three "tercios" or thirds: Varas, Banderillas, Muerte (Death).

Tienta – Testing of the cows for bravery in the open countryside, used for breeding *bravo* bulls.

Toreo – The training and art of being a bullfighter. Practice.

Torero/a – Describes anyone in the team employed by the matador. (Literally means Bullman, suggesting a trade.)

Traje de Luces – Also referred to as "traje". Literally, "suit of lights" The outfit the matador wears trimmed in gold or sometimes black. The suits worn by the cuadrilla are trimmed in silver; these men are sometimes called "hombres de plata", or "men of silver".

Trapio – The quality grading of the bull, the breeding. Used to describe how brave and strong the bull comes out, and how he performs in the bullring, but also how he looks according to his breeding.

Vara – The spear used by the picador.

Contacts

Anti-bullfighting

ALF – Animal Liberation Front, known in the media for their fundamentalist and sometimes illegal approach to animal activism. They practice direct action and campaign effectively online with targeted campaigns. Zero tolerance approach to any animal cruelty including bullfighting. www.animalliberationfront.com

League Against Cruel Sports – Direct action and campaigning group against any bloodsport, generalising by including bullfighting in their agenda. They campaign with big brands and petition support to stop subsidies for bullfighting. www.league.org.uk

Equanimal – Animal Rights Activists in Spain. Naked protestors. Direct action at bullfights including disruption and blockade work. Peaceful protesting. www.equanimal.org

Prou – Platform that collected the signatures to ban bullfighting in Catalonia. www.prou.cat

Mercy For Animals – Organisation based in the US who campaign against factory farming and cruelty to animals by undercover camera work and more. www.mercyforanimals.org

Pro-bullfighting

Federacion de Entidades Taurinas de Catalunya – The Catalan organisation for taurine businesses and related organisations working to overturn the Catalan ban on bullfighting. Marilén Barceló Verea is vice president. www.federaciotaurinadecatalunya.es

Club Taurino London UK – A group of aficionados meeting in Spain and UK for bullfighting related dinners and social activities. Provide a font of knowledge for beginner aficionados in the form of literature and DVDs. Membership enquiries: www.ctol.org

MundoToro – A Spanish language website with latest news on bullfighting. www.mundotoro.com

TaquillaToros – Tickets portal and news in English and Spanish. www.ticktackticket.com/entradas

Rivera Ordóñez – Official Francisco Rivera Ordóñez website. www.riveraordonez.com

Catalonia Links

Generalitat de Catalunya – More about the current news in politics. www.gencat.cat

History of bullfighting in Catalonia. es.wikipedia.org/wiki/Tauromaquia_en_Cataluña

Geography and regional information on Catalonia. www.photius.com/countries/spain/society/spain_society _the_catalans.html

Further Reading

Jason Webster
Or The Bull Kills You, Chatto & Windus

Alexander Fiske-Harrison
Into The Arena, Profile Books

Antoni Strubell
What Catalans Want, Catalonia Press

Alfred Bosch
I ara què?, Galaxia Gutemberg

Frank Evans
The Last British Bullfighter, Macmillan

Marilén Barceló Verea
Mano a Mano, Visionnet

Edward Lewine
Death And The Sun, Doubleday

Federico Garcia Lorca
In Search of Duende, New Directions Publishing

Thanks

I have many people to thank for this book and the film, The Bull and The Ban. Señor Bob, my best man on the job, who unfailingly was the best assistant producer anyone could ask for. Thanks to Gina for allowing me to bug him so often! Thanks to the CTL, in particular Ivan Moseley. This project would not have happened at all without you. Noel Chandler was a star for arranging the best meetings and just generally accepting me into the upper echelons without question. Kitty Witwer, for woman-type support in a world of men, and again the best connections in the taurine world (You- are- very- kind!) Catalan Parliament for getting me the footage, Mercy For Animals, Prou and Equanimal likewise, also for trusting I would represent you well, I hope I have. Jason Webster for coming to get us when we were stranded in the "African Sex Quarter". Anna Maria and Graham for your translation and connections. Bruno and Isabel for subtitles. Fran Rivera Ordóñez for even agreeing to do it, besos. Fernando Cámara Castro for all the support and wonderful open words from all, you have some stars, particularly thanks to Mario, Emilio and Lazaro. Los Corchos in Fuengirola for allowing filming. And special thanks to Julio De La Puerta and family for taking the time to show this odd Englishwoman around your wonderful finca. And finally, Pete for putting up with my ridiculous ideas. And thanks to my dad for planting a seed of my passion for Spain when you brought home the Spanish "comb" and flamenco dolls from Cadiz; the seed grew!

The Bull and The Ban

About the Author

Catherine Tosko worked in the magazine industry in London as an editor before making several short films. "The Bull and The Ban" was her first full length documentary, which she filmed, directed, produced and edited herself. She is also an accomplished artist, photographer and tattooist and has studied at Stanford University, USA and London Guildhall University in software and IT related subjects, as well as being a qualified English Language teacher from Clare College Cambridge. She lives in Andalusia with her husband and their pets and is mother to twin boys.

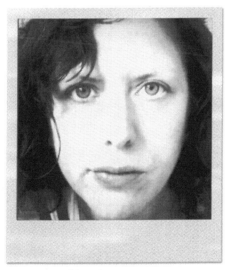

Catherine Tosko

The Bull and The Ban

2841897R00100

Printed in Great Britain
by Amazon.co.uk, Ltd.,
Marston Gate.